SECRETS OF SUCCESSFUL

Carl E. Bolte, Jr.

ARCO PUBLISHING, INC.
NEW YORK

Greater love have no parents than Carl and Muriel
who listened to years of wrong notes.
To them this book is fondly dedicated.

Published by Arco Publishing, Inc.
215 Park Avenue South, New York, N.Y. 10003

Library of Congress Cataloging in Publication Data

Bolte, Carl E., 1929–
    Secrets of successful songwriting.

    Previous ed. published in 1978 as: Successful
songwriting.
    1. Music, Popular (Songs, etc.)—Writing and
publishing.   I. Bolte, Carl E., 1929–   . Successful
songwriting.   II. Title.
MT67.B56   1984   784.5'0028   84-6391
ISBN 0-668-06170-7 (pbk.)

Printed in the United States of America

10   9   8   7   6   5   4   3   2   1

TABLE OF CONTENTS

FOREWORD

Carl Bolte, Jr., is eminently qualified to provide you with a springboard into the songwriting waters which can seem murky and formidable to the uninitiated. In easily understood style, he offers that essential "how to" information which is invaluable to all songwriters, beginners or professionals.

In addition to his obvious and often-recognized compositional talents (he also wrote *Marilyn. . . The Most*, Marilyn Maye's first LP), he has written some two dozen plays (including the first *Give 'Em Hell, Harry!*), and has taught courses on popular songwriting at the highly respected Conservatory of Music in Kansas City.

This is a book written by a man who is a songwriter and a teacher, who knows the songwriting industry, and who is sufficiently down-to-earth to translate theory into practical step-by-step application.

Secrets of Successful Songwriting should certainly improve your creative ability. The ideas, programs, and suggestions you find here will come as close as anything possibly could to assuring your success in the songwriting field.

There is nothing in these pages of the secret elixir and the magic formula, because there are none when it comes to the writing of songs. What this book, however, will do for the sincere aspirant is to show, in easily understood and entertaining fashion, exactly how to begin, how to polish, and, finally, to many of us perhaps most importantly, how to market.

Ralph Blane

PREFACE

Information contained in *Secrets of Successful Songwriting* has nearly as many sources as there are colors in the rainbow. You will find facts, opinions, observations, examples, and analyses of songs which are—and continue to be—the best in popular music.

Absent are current on-the-chart tunes. Why? We will be discussing songs which have remained favorites through several decades and entertained perhaps three generations. They are standards, musical proof of continued success, and not a here-today-gone-tomorrow tuneful fad.

Our scope is limited strictly to popular music. It will include other song types written for a special purpose: marches, patriotic numbers, fraternity songs, show tunes. If those composers did not write only with the "pop" market in mind, their songs have enjoyed wide acclaim. We will study them to determine how and why they found success, remained popular through the years, and learn from their attributes.

Stephen Collins Foster was one of America's all-time popular composers. He entertained audiences a century ago. The public desires in music change, just as do our tastes in other fields. Therefore, our reference will include only songs written since the 1920s.

Emphasis will be on the forms which successful songwriters have employed. You will not find a quick formula for overnight hit status because there is no such cut-and-dried recipe. You will see a certain conformity and commonality regarding popular song characteristics in their many categories of titles, lyrics, melodies, and others.

There are exceptions—many of them—to be sure. While we will concentrate on songs which adhere to the more universal patterns (and that is the vast majority of popular songs), we will discuss the exceptions to illustrate that no format is all-conclusive.

The examples chosen because of their special content come from one or more of the following sources and criteria:

1. Songs which achieved top national recognition on "Your Hit Parade." This radio/television program was sponsored by Lucky Strike cigarettes and presented by the American Tobacco Company from April 20, 1935, through June 7, 1958.
2. A survey taken of some 150 people in various age, race, income, marital, religious, and occupational categories.
3. Songs which are hits, perennial standards, and otherwise memorable to the author in his forty years of appreciative listening, performing, composing, and teaching.
4. We follow a simple truth: America applauded them, and we quote the contents of these songs which make them dear to our hearts.

All of these songs will be informative and illustrative. None were picked because of personal favoritism. Any advocacy or protagonism is strictly based on its aid to you.

A songwriter has a simple premise: provide what the listening public wants, needs, and accepts. By our scrutiny of these songs, we hope to find their secrets, so that you can enjoy that same fame and fortune.

We hasten to state that there is no way to teach a non-songwriter to write songs. Either we have that creative ability or we don't. We can, however, help every songwriter become a better songwriter. That is the sole purpose of this book.

Our findings are based on songs which have been musical hits. They may be an artistic triumph (such as "Stella by Starlight" and "Gone with the Wind" which are often referred to as "musicians' songs" because they are appreciated by performers) or a financial success. The ultimate goal, if it is your goal, is that your music will be both.

The writing of *Secrets of Successful Songwriting* has been a challenging and thrilling experience. It has been a two-year happy association with the best of American popular music, an almost-personal acquaintanceship with our outstanding composers and lyricists, and a better understanding of their magnificent creative efforts.

We hope that you will enjoy *Secrets of Successful Songwriting*. It is a great pleasure to share this exciting field with you, to offer helpful hints, and to salute your talent. Our desire is that you will become a Hit Parader, a Top-Charter, a musical household word, and have fun with your music.

Yours in the fun and fellowship of popular music creativity,

Carl E. Bolte, Jr.

GRATEFUL ACKNOWLEDGMENTS

Where do we start? There is no "first of all" because all of you are first. Neither is there "last but not least." And so, in alphabetical order, let me express to each of you very warm thanks.

For Getting It in Print

To two of America's songwriting best—Ralph Blane and Irving Caesar—for their gracious sponsorship and generous opening remarks.

To Kenneth W. Heady, for sharing his alliterative poem, "December's Dart."

To Charles B. Kauffman, National Director of Communications, Boy Scouts of America, for information on "God Bless America."

To Michael A. Mardikes, Dean of the Conservatory of Music, University of Missouri at Kansas City, for his invaluable help, and for letting me share the joy of teaching as a member of his faculty.

To Lieutenant Commander Charlie Plumb, USNR, author of *I'm No Hero*, for his get-it-published professional assistance.

To Nancy Rosenthal of ASCAP, Patrick J. Fabbio of BMI, and Lewis M. Bachman of AGAC for many answers to many questions.

To David R. Smalley, whose legal expertise, advice, and friendship in and outside the covers of this book are limitless.

To Mrs. Emelyn Swisher, for her translation, suggestions, and patient retyping of the retypings.

To the American Tobacco Company, a division of American Brands, Inc., for permission to quote from the survey of their outstanding radio/television program, "Your Hit Parade."

For Patient Help on the Romantic Musical Road

To Miss Rebecca Birch who started it all with "Now play this, little man" to a four-year-old. Bless you, "Birchie."

To "Dutch" Whalen and Tommy Foster, for making the step from the classics to popular piano a pleasant one.

To the late Professor Claude Fichthorne, Dean of the School of Music at Missouri Valley College. Rest you peacefully, sir.

To John Willer, for his demands on the worst flute and piccolo player ever to come under his band-leading tutelage.

And Others in the Musical Faith

To bandleaders who let me perform.

To the parishioners of the First Baptist Church in Slater, Missouri, who maintained a pious attitude in spite of my early organ efforts.

To the sidemen on my bandstands who experimented with my tunes and arrangements, and were even occasionally complimentary.

To the students of my Popular Songwriting classes for being a sounding board.

To survey "subscribers" for reporting their opinions of our best popular songs.

To all of you, thanks for your invaluable contributions. Part of you lies within these pages.

Repay these important friends I can't. Hopefully their thanks will come from passing along their inspirational information to you, the reader.

INTRODUCTION

TAKE IT FROM THE TOP, AND TAKE IT FROM CARL!

You are fortunate to have such a mentor as my friend. Carl E. Bolte, Jr., is an authority in our field. Read *Secrets of Successful Songwriting,* and practice his advice. What Carl says here, he says with complete reliability.

He is an avid student on the subject. His dynamic instruction has helped many fledgling composers as he teaches session after session in Popular Songwriting and Composition at the Conservatory of Music at the University of Missouri at Kansas City. In addition, he continues to be a practicing and prolific songwriter.

Because he needed a text to guide our future songwriters, Carl wrote it. His information is based on personal experience in his twenty-five years in our kind of music. He analyzed not just what it takes to be "on the charts" but what the requirements are to have on-the-chart hits remain as standards through the years. In no uncertain terms he tells you why they are, and provides his insight. You will find no equivocation; you will find a clear-cut edict for making your song a continuing musical legend. I like the dimensions he specifies in his adamant rules for your understanding.

Read *Secrets of Successful Songwriting,* then keep it handy. In every song you write, check its contents against his advice. His book has only one objective: to make you better and more knowledgeable songwriters.

May you find that same pleasant experience which has been my good fortune with "Tea for Two"!

I wish you well.

Irving Caesar

A. IN THE BEGINNING

CHAPTER ONE

THE SONGWRITING PROFESSION
or Hello, Fellow Cockeyed Optimists!

Welcome to the world of the unknown! It is a never-never land of unpredictables. There is not one single factor on which we can hang our security or plot a guaranteed course for success. It is truly a jungle all its own. Yet in spite of all these logical reasons for our not being in it, we are...because it is the ever-ever territory of inviting, creative excitement!

Necessities for belonging to our great songwriting fraternity are few. We must have inventive talent. With it, we need a crystal ball, cup-runneth-over luck, and the uncanny, unscientific, unprescribed good fortune of being in the right place with the right material at the right time. (Didn't we say that the specific formula for triumph has no landmarks?)

Compare those scant and frail necessities with other professions. For instance, if you want to be a lawyer, you graduate from law school, hang out your shingle, and you are in business. All of a sudden you are the finest practicing attorney in Shipwreck, Missouri.

Now relate that occupational route to songwriting. Nobody in the music world cares if you are the best tunesmith in your community. Of course, that recognition is good for your ego. But to be a successful composer, you must rank among the dozen-or-so best in the country. We don't compete only in Shipwreck, or Missouri, or the midwest. We place our best creative efforts against international competitors because the market for our wares is worldwide. We face tough odds in writing hit songs to make the Top Forty Chart.

They say that the most fervent optimists, by virtue of their career callings, are preachers, playwrights, and prospectors. Add one more: we songwriters. Studies show that less than one of every hundred songs written gets published. If we are not willing to

1

accept the courteous reply of "sorry but no thanks" on the first ninety-nine songs we submit to music publishers, smile and write our next magnificent tune, and keep at it until somebody finally recognizes the genius which we have displayed all along, then we should go back to the farm instead of the piano.

This is by no means meant to discourage you. We repeat that you must have talent—real ability—and be at the right place at the right time with the right material in the music market.

In our Conservatory class on Popular Songwriting, we analyze student songs on the same criteria which you will find here. It is based not only on what ingredients make up a hit song, but we take it a giant step further: What has made that song a standard to live through the years? Students are quick to point out that today's top tunes are not as confined and structured as were songs in the earlier eras of "Stardust," "Night and Day," and "White Christmas." However, they just as promptly determine that those same rules remain valid now, even if the current songs have a few more exceptions and fewer restrictions.

Before we place the art of songwriting into science, and/or elevate the science of songwriting into an art (and perhaps it is both), we realize that widespread popular appeal of your material may not be your goal. If you wrote your song for your own pleasure, that is a reward in itself. Play it. Show it proudly to your friends. Enjoy your personal accomplishment: you *are* a songwriter.

Perhaps you wrote your song for Shirley. Perform it for her, pouring your heart into your special music and lyrics. Both of you will be delighted. That is true creative achievement.

If either of these is your final objective, the suggestions in this book will help you write better songs...for your own self-satisfaction or for Shirley.

If your goal is fame and fortune in popular music, *Successful Songwriting* will aid you in achieving it.

To state that there are rules in songwriting is to oversimplify. If you write a melody and lyrics, that is a song. There are no exact measuring devices to tell which song will attain top recognition, but there are rules if you want to be financially successful. These rules might be better termed "analyses" or "findings" or "statistical results." If you will accept that explanation (which is admittedly too strong a definition), we offer our cold-fact studied approach.

Why are there songwriting guidelines? How can we contain the free creativity of songwriting within a restrictive framework? Must the song written for Shirley have any constraints? Who can tell a songwriter how to put his personal magic into his music?

We can't and won't. We urge you to write anything you desire. But if your aim is hit status in the music market, we propose some parameters to help you understand the proper framework which has been acceptable to the music-buying public. Now that we have made that supposition—that as long as you are a music creator, it would be nice to enjoy further rewards—we propose these axioms.

Since you are writing that chart-busting song to be heard over the airwaves and become a household word that will be enjoyed on the bandstand and requested on the dance floor for generations to make you an international VIP and take you to the bank twice a day, then this is exactly what you are creating:

Finding a short, catchy, appealing title;

Repeating that title often in your song;

Composing an easy-to-remember melody;

Writing can't-miss nicely-rhyming lyrics;

Using the AABA/ABAC/ABABAB formats;

Scoring in an easy and playable key;

Keeping your melody within a singable range;

Copyrighting your masterpiece;

Placing it in the proper market channels.

There is one more criterion that won't appear in our analyses and findings and statistics. We will repeat it again and again throughout these pages. It is the best test of all—the ear test. It simply means what your ear "hears" regarding your song. And "ear" includes the broad physiology of heart, mind, and soul. If your "ear" likes it, your song has merit. Every hit song has passed that primary critical test.

We know of no other field where the working toward success is quite as exciting as in the discipline of popular music. If "arriving" is half the fun of achieving that status through the creation of songs, then it is worth pursuing. Fame and fortune belong to a few; but there are no losers among the creative, because we have created.

Read on from here, fellow songwriter. If you will supply the imaginative and inventive talent, we'll provide some helpful hints. We wrote this book for you, and welcome you as you join us musical cockeyed optimists.

CHAPTER TWO

"WRITE" THE SONGS YOU WRITE
or Draw a Musical Map

In our Conservatory class was a gifted young composer. He was always coming up with attractive and fresh melodies. But he had a problem: he had no idea of how to put the tune in his head onto paper. Whenever he wrote a song, he needed someone to "chart" it for him. He wasn't alone. Others faced the same dilemma.

We set out to answer his need. We played middle C on the piano, followed by E above it, a three-note interval. Did he recognize the difference? Yes; the second note was higher. How much higher he wasn't sure, but it was higher.

Then we played middle C, and C an octave above. He knew that these two notes had a greater range/space than the first example. That, too, was progress.

All students were given a blank sheet of paper. We sounded a note on the piano, then hit a note at random above it. Each student made a mark for the starting note, another for the second note. We followed with several more notes, some higher, some lower; they logged their papers accordingly. We then made it more difficult by hitting notes at half-step intervals. They marked their papers, but it wasn't easy.

By now, as you can imagine, every non-"writing" songwriter had a messy page which looked like a poor exercise in graph-making.

On clean paper, we repeated this process several times. With each exercise the students began to put the notes in the proper range and interval. With no reference point except that which they devised themselves (some had notes in a four-inch vertical array), they placed them accurately above and below the original note. That may not seem like a breakthrough to you, but it was an important advance for them.

With that understanding of note relationships, we introduced them to the musical staff. On manuscript paper we identified by letter/name the line or space which each note occupies. They quickly saw that this was a framework for what they had been

5

placing on blank paper; now it had specific boundaries and positions.

If improvement was obvious, total understanding was yet to come. Another student needed more help. Were there examples of note intervals in hit tunes? Yes. We made a list of songs. That was a real assist to the class, something to which they could relate. Here it is for your interest:[1]

First Note	First Different Note	Interval	Musical Term	Song
C^2	D	no notes	a 2nd	"It Might as Well Be Spring"
C	E	1 note	a 3rd	"Have Yourself a Merry Little Christmas"
C	F	2 notes	a 4th	"All the Things You Are"
C	G	3 notes	a 5th	"People Will Say We're in Love"
C^2	A	4 notes	a 6th	"That Old Black Magic"
C	B	5 notes	a 7th	none
C	C	6 notes	an octave	"Over the Rainbow"

Then we required that time values be given to notes. That was an equally painful process, but within weeks each composer was scoring his songs. His efforts were primitive; probably no other music reader could play his lead sheet. Rhythm was askew, note-time values were doubtful, and measures in 4/4 time ranged from 2/4 through something approaching 13/4, give or take a few beats. Nonetheless, he was—at least for his own satisfaction—a song-"writer." It made sense to him. It was his song. He could play it. (To learn more about this exercise, see chapter 25, "Time Values.")

We encouraged this progress. Soon every student improved his accuracy so that other class members could also play his songs.

---

1. For ease of understanding, we transposed and assumed all songs to have a universal lead/starting note of C.

2. Starting/lead note is a pickup note.

You too can learn to write your songs on manuscript paper just as these students did. Try this same approach. It is not as difficult as you think. Instruction guides at your library will be of help.

A friend of mine is a non-"writing" songwriter. He composed a one-act musical comedy. It took us five different lunch sessions. He whistled and sang; I ate and wrote his twelve-tune score into the proper form. In spite of the gravy stains, his musical was a success!

And a further example. . . I wish I could recall his name, because he has had songs on the charts. He graduated from Ol' Miss, worked in his father's drugstore, and played the radio all day to cut down the boredom. With the ability to compose and after a year of pushing pills, he had a dozen tunes in his head, all of which followed the song forms he heard on the radio. He went to Los Angeles, found a musician to chart his songs while he sang them, and made his mark in popular music about 1959.

These examples point out that it is not critical that you learn to score your own songs. They also clearly prove that you can avoid error by the "middleman," save the time and effort and expense of a musical stenographer, and know that what is on paper is your song. . . because *you* put it there.

CHAPTER THREE

TOOLS
or Here Is Help with Your Homework

Songwriters need only a few assisting aids. We have that one all-important necessity—the unique creative ability to compose melodies and write lyrics. But we can make our pleasant task better and easier. These tools are simple but very specific requirements.

First, paper, musical manuscripts, and pencils. They should be available everywhere you are—at your piano, your bedside, in your car, your desk, your hobby workbench, and always in your pocket. Yes, even in your bathroom.[1] Carry a scratchpad when you are working in your garden; the distance from backyard to desk might as well be miles if you lose that inspired idea before you can write it down.

Second, a tape recorder. Have you ever composed a melody, only to have the first four bars vanish while you were playing the next four bars? Had you recorded it, it would still be there. Although what you hear when you play it back may be unfinished and need additional efforts to polish it, you can capture that original idea, that real gem of inspirational creativity, which is too often lost. When that magic is gone, a song tends to sound more like the product of craftsmanship than the genius of an artist. As you compose, do so into your tape recorder—even with the wordless hums, your personal comments and explanations, and singing "la-la-la" because your words aren't yet complete (whose are on the first attempt?). Finish your song later; retain that initial spark by recording it.

Keep not one but *two* tape recorders. Place one on your desk, piano, or whatever where you usually compose. Put the second at your bedside so that you won't miss that late-at-night inspiration.

---

1. Covered with soapsuds and a towel, I emerged halfway through a shower aboard the aircraft carrier USS *Ticonderoga* in 1971 to write three pages of lyrics. Inspiration can and does strike us at any and all times.

Third, a piano, guitar, or other instrument. While many songwriters compose without instrumental help because they can do so by "hearing" it, your instrument should be available. To be sure that your mental "ear" is correct, use it to make the minor adjustments in the melody line and chords.

Fourth, a dictionary and a rhyming dictionary. They will help you find that one right word to write it right now (see chapter 12, "Rhyming").

Fifth, a work sheet. The song, "Pretty You!", following, has its work sheet with it. Study both. Here is a translation of it:

A. **Rhythm/Bar Count.** It is exactly that—the number of beats and measures which comprise each lyric line of two musical bars. At the end of each phrase of four lyric lines is the total number of bars. You can be sure that your group of lyrics adds up to eight measures.

B. **Syl.** The abbreviation for "syllables." Since "Pretty You!" is an AABA song, you will see that the number of syllables in line one in each "A" phrase are identical. This also applies to each of the other three lines in every "A" section.

C. Because more thought was needed as to the best lyric of two possibilities, there are ( ) around "Lucky me!" and "Handsome me!" Those ( ) show a choice to make, remind you to review it and ultimately pick the better phrase. This was done by drawing a line through "Handsome me!" Note that "Handsome me!" was deleted, yet was left visible for a final afterthought reconsideration. The ( ) are then removed from the "keeper" words "Lucky me!"

D. This denotes the bridge, so it won't be confused with the "A" phrases. Of course, the bridge is not repeated, either in words or music, and does not need a musical yardstick. It is labeled for the songwriter's information.

E. This notation affirms that it is a tag, not to be mistaken with any other portion of the song structure.

F. A final checklist will let the composer study his song and its comparative conformity to the general rules of popular hits. In "Pretty You!" we find that . . .

1. Lyrics consist of 95 words.

2. Form is AABA (t), the "(t)" indicating a tag ending.

3. Title: "corner, 2 words, tag, 4 times." These remarks explain that the title is "up in the corner," or the first words of the lyrics; it contains two words; it is repeated in the tag; and the title is stated a total of four times.

4. Melodic range is a 10th, or middle C to E an octave above.

5. There are eleven different chords used.

6. It is written in the key of C.

7. There are thirty-two bars, a four-bar tag, for a total of thirty-six bars.

8. It is played in 4/4 time.

9. The "A" has a 1, 1, X, 1 rhyme scheme with "me" being its rhyming sound. The "B" (bridge) has a 1a/1b, 2, 3a/3b, 2 rhyme scheme, with "near," "day," and "belong" rhyming sounds. The last item shows that line three rhymes with line three in every "A" phrase.

G. This is the "composer's corner." Notes to yourself might include such items as © applied for on _____, © received on _____, make demo at _____ on _____, with these musicians _____, send demo to _____, ask _____for best group to record it, etc.

H. Mark your work sheet with this copyright legend exactly as it appears. Do so when you apply for your copyright, even though its official acknowledgment has not been received from the Library of Congress (see chapter 28, "Copyright").

You will note that the lyrics are double-spaced, with triple-spacing between each phrase containing eight bars of lyrics. Spacing between words on each horizontal line of the lyrics is wider than normal. That additional room will allow you to make changes if you wish.

By utilizing this work sheet, you can analyze virtually everything about your song. It is a valuable assist which will help you construct your songs, and provide a final analysis of necessary requirements which have spelled *success* behind other composers' names.

Many of the items regarding song content mentioned here may be new to you. They will be fully explained in following chapters.

Use all of these tools. They will be of real benefit to you. And in our exciting but unmapped songwriting "jungle," we need all the help we can get!

Good news! The "worksheet" is now available. In high-quality professional form, the SONGWRITERS CREATIVE MATRIX is the only assistance of this kind ever offered specifically for songwriters. It contains instructions, explanations, examples, and twenty-five MATRIX guidance forms for your immediate use. Send $12.50 (plus tax for Missouri residents), which includes handling, postage, and insurance to Holly Productions, Department B, 800 Greenway Terrace, Kansas City, Missouri 64113.

PRETTY YOU!

Words/Music:
Carl E. Bolte, Jr.
800 Greenway Terrace
Kansas City, Mo. 64113

Words/music by: **Carl E. Bolte, Jr. — ASCAP**
Address: **800 Greenway Terrace**
City/State/Zip: **Kansas City, Mo. 64113**
Phone: **(816) 931-2248/756-0266**
Date: **September 4, 1975**

TITLE: _____ **PRETTY YOU!** _____

rhythm/bar count (A)	syl (B)	lyrics
‖‖ ‖‖	6	PRETTY YOU! ⚹ Lucky me! ⚹ (Handsome me!) (C)
‖‖ ‖‖	8	We're as happy as we can be.
‖‖ ‖‖	7	Nothing matters: we have us …
‖‖ ‖‖	6	It suits us to a 'T'.

(subtotal: __8__ bars)

‖‖ ‖‖	6	PRETTY YOU! ⚹ Lucky me! ⚹ (Handsome me!) (C)
‖‖ ‖‖	8	Our whole world is a joy to see.
‖‖ ‖‖	7	Got no troubles, we don't fuss
‖‖ ‖‖	6	'Cause we're good company.

(subtotal: __16__ bars)

		(bridge) (D)
‖‖ ‖‖	8	You are near, and it's clear why the
‖‖ ‖‖	5	Sun shines ev'ry day.
‖‖ ‖‖	8	We belong; nothing can go wrong …
‖‖ ‖‖	10	I'll keep you here to stay with me. 'Cause you're

(subtotal: __24__ bars)

‖‖ ‖‖	6	PRETTY YOU! ⚹ Lucky me! ⚹ (Handsome me!) (C)
‖‖ ‖‖	8	We're as easy as A B C.
‖‖ ‖‖	7	Not a problem to discuss:
‖‖ ‖‖	6	We're perfect harmony.

(subtotal/total: __32__ bars)

tag if any: (E)

‖‖ ‖‖	3	PRETTY YOU! (C)
‖‖ ‖‖	3	⚹ Lucky me! ⚹ (Handsome me!)

Total: __4 bars = 36__ bars

Comments/notes: (G)

Check-List analysis: (F)

words:	95
form:	AABA(t)
title:	corner, 2 words, tag, 4 times
range:	10th
chords:	11
key:	C
bars:	32 + 4 tag = 36
time:	4/4
rhyme/sound:	A = 1,1,x,1 (me)
	B = 1a/1b,2,3a/3b/2
	(near, day, belong)
	A = line 3 rhyme (us)

13

CHAPTER FOUR

COLLABORATE AND CELEBRATE!
or Should I Share My Pie with the Other Guy?

This subject might also be titled, "Brother, can you spare a helping hand?" to paraphrase an old song.

Do you need a collaborator, a music/lyric partner? It is a good question, and it has a simple solution. If you don't write both words and music, you need a creative teammate. If you possess those abilities, you are capable of going the songwriting profession alone. . . probably.

Note that we said "probably." Even if you are dual-talented, there is always the opportunity to profit from a fresh approach by your co-writer. With few exceptions, most songwriters collaborated on hit songs at some point in their distinguished careers.

The writing of a musical score, more often than not, has collaborative talents. The requirement of composing some eighteen or more songs seems most successful by two (and sometimes three) people. The reason is clear: two heads are better than one in assuring that every song is original and nonrepetitive. That demanding assignment can often best be accomplished by the check and balance of teamwork. (See chapter 27, "Writing a Musical Stage Score.")

The spoils which belong to the musically creative victors are obviously diminished in collaboration. Yet the chances of enjoying these rewards are greater when songwriters team up. Each musical "lone ranger" gets help with new ideas, a fresh approach, perhaps more originality in melody and lyrics, and a critique by his partner. With teamwork songwriters can avoid having an Act II song sound like a warmed-over version of a tune in Act I.

This list is by no means pure nor complete. Many lyricists have worked with other composers than those stated, and vice versa. Here are creative combinations which have made musical history: Rodgers and Hart; Rodgers and Hammerstein; Lerner and Loewe; Martin and Blane; Ross and Adler; Harnick and Bock; Jones and

Schmidt; Brown and Henderson and DeSilva; Fields and Comden and Green; Ebb and Kander; Harburg and Lane; Gordon and Revel; Adamson and McHugh; Burke and VanHeusen; Gershwin and Gershwin; Mercer and Arlen; Cahn and Styne; Kahn and Kern; Dietz and Schwartz; Newley and Bricusse.

Some of the superb men of music also had an infrequent collaborator. They are generally recognized for songs in which they wrote both words and music. They are familiar to every listener—Berlin, Porter Loesser, Weill, Foster, Kahn, Willson, Herman, Rome, Coots, Ellington, Carmichael.

The personal relationships and professional experiences of these songwriting teams are interesting.

John Kander and Fred Ebb are an outstanding example of collaboration success. Their triumphs are well known: *Cabaret*, *Zorba*, *Chicago*, *Flora*, *the Red Menace*, and *70, Girls, 70*.

Temperament can be a real issue in collaboration. Gilbert and Sullivan could not abide each other, yet each recognized the immense ability of his partner. They avoided personal friction, and for years worked "together" only by mail to achieve continued international fame; Gilbert sent lyrics to Sullivan who set them to music.

The Kander-Ebb team has had no such difficulties. So close is their professional harmony that in more than a dozen years they've never had a serious difference.

Collaboration techniques differ with each team. The Kander-Ebb combine is careful not to submit a finished melody or lyric to the other for fear of conscripting that partner into a restrictive form.

Such was not the case with Oscar Hammerstein II. In the earlier years of his career, he set his words to already composed music by Kern, Romberg, Friml, and Youmans. This practice was reversed and the lyric came first on some of the classics while he worked with Richard Rodgers on *Oklahoma!* After that triumph, the Rodgers-Hammerstein successful formula was either approach: write music or lyrics initially, depending only on inspiration.

Regarding his partnership with Hammerstein, Richard Rodgers said that neither would have benefited much from the association unless they had shared a healthy respect "for the nature and problems of the other's medium, a happy willingness to bend before the other's working needs."

Hammerstein said that Rodgers was not one to praise excessively. However, Hammerstein seemed contented when, upon presenting to Rodgers lyrics to a melody, the latter said, "It fits."

Study the techniques and experiences of these great songwriting teams. They will be a help if collaboration is for you.

Should you decide to collaborate, you will be wise to have a mutual understanding. The happy atmosphere is fun as you both commence your talented joint operation. That pleasure can dissipate into dissonance when your song becomes a hit and money enters the picture. Take time to draw up a clear and definite agreement at the very beginning to avoid differences of opinion, the loss of friendship, and even legal hassles later.

Items to be included in such a document are:

1. *Ownership.* Do both collaborators own it, share and share alike, 50/50? Did one partner write the music only, and he alone owns the melody? Is that also true of the lyricist and his lyrics? Did both partners contribute more or less equally to both words and music? Who owns what?

2. *Contract spokesman.* Which partner has the power to negotiate a binding contract with a producer?

3. *Authority to make changes.* What if a publisher wants to alter a part of the song? Who has the right to do so, on words and/or music? If both collaborators are required to agree, what happens if they don't?

4. *Permission for commercial jingles.* This use of musical standards is in ever-increasing demand in the advertising industry. Generally the practice is to write "commercial" lyrics to a classic pop tune. Who has the authority to permit it? Do both partners share in the proceeds of such an agreement? If so, on what percentage basis?

5. *Management.* Who collects and distributes royalties, answers correspondence, and otherwise makes decisions about the song for the benefit of both collaborators?

6. *A buy-sell agreement.* This clause should definitely be

included because these possibilities can arise:

a. Suppose one partner needs cash for some specific purpose. Rather than hold legal proceedings, a pre-determined basis/price will establish each partner's value and avoid haggling difficulties and delays. (Such buy-sell agreements are often based on X times the latest, or average, annual net income earned by the song.)

b. Suppose both collaborators have agreed on a 50/50 ownership. One partner dies, leaving five equal-sharing heirs to his property, which includes your song. This clause would allow the surviving partner to pay the estate an established figure instead of having to negotiate with each of the five heirs over every decision regarding the song. (Rather than having an expensive, time-consuming lawsuit, the American Arbitration Association* is available to you should such difficulties arise.)

This subject is not meant to alarm you. Nor is it necessary to dial "L" for lawyer when a longtime songwriting friend suggests that you join him in composition. But it is recommended that you have a gentleman's agreement which is mutually understood to avoid hardship and heartache later.

A collaborator and I made such an arrangement on a song. We arrived on a percentage share of any proceeds received after all costs were paid. We broke it down into what we felt each area of participation toward the total song was worth in future income, as follows:

---

*Your author is proud to be a member of this fine organization which has fairly and equitably settled many disputes out of court.

Contribution	Mac	Carl
Original song idea	10%	0%
Majority of tune/lyrics	15%	5%
Financing (demos, clerical, mail, other)	0%	50%
All promotion activities	0%	20%
Totals	25%	75%

We further agreed that I had total authority in any and all matters concerning our song. We did not have a buy-sell agreement. Writing this chapter reminds me that such an instrument is necessary between us. Fortunately, it is not too late to obtain one, and this will be done to protect both of us, our heirs, and our friendship.

Be your own judge. If you write both words and music and would rather travel the songwriting road alone, collaboration is not for you. You can always change your mind for help on future songs. Get in harness with a composer or lyricist if you need some assistance, now or in the future.

Remember: half a pie is better than none.

B. I CHRISTEN THEE

CHAPTER FIVE

SONG TITLES
or Give Your New Baby a Nice Name

Congratulations! You have written a song! You are the proud new parent of a musical entity which was not here yesterday. Nobody could write your song but you. It's a great feeling, isn't it? You deserve our applause.

What are you going to call it? As with a new baby, its name isn't its most important consideration. The characteristics of soul and personality and beauty are. The same is true with the song. Even if it has great ingredients, a good name will still be a help. Just as you give a baby a head start with a decent name, you also do so with a song.

Think of these images. Suppose a baby is named Mushmouth Jones, or Garbage Smith, or Trashy Brown, or Average Johnson. Two things happen as we envision this funny-named baby-person:

1. It is so unique that the creature bearing this "handle" must be very unusual, and that can be either good or bad.
2. It is offensive, and immediately we do not want to know him.

On the other hand, we are attracted to Winner Eastman, Happy Grant, and Victorious Kelly.

Note the difference in these names. They are conventional, yet each has a varying connotation. Compare and consider them:

JOHN/SUSAN - formal, very proper.
JOHNNY/SUSIE - casual, cute, clever.
The same is true with ROBERT/BOBBY or REBECCA/BECKY.

Now check your mental vision with these nicknames: BOOTS, BUTCH, DUTCH, KITTY, SLIM, DUKE, SPEEDY, LEFTY, FLASH, ACE, SKIPPER, CAT, BABY, RAINBOW, PAPA, BOSS.

The picture you get from each tends to make you want to know

19

them, or not. That title/name, whether for a song or person, *is* important.[1]

Where do we get good titles? Virtually every place. Consider these sources:

1. Old sayings: "Look for a Silver Lining," "All That Glitters Is Not Gold."
2. Romantic phrases: "I Love You," "You're My Everything."
3. Endearing words: "Babyface," "Honey," "Let Me Call You Sweetheart," "My Darling."
4. Greetings/departings: "Goodbye"; "Have a Nice Day"; "Hey, There"; "Good Morning, My Dear."
5. Patriotic phrases: "God Bless America," "Praise the Lord and Pass the Ammunition," "Anchors Aweigh!"
6. Conversation:[2] "What's New?" "Fine and Dandy," "You're the Top."
7. The media: radio, television, and publications. A standard or catchy phrase from these sources has been turned into hit tunes. Examples: "Good News," "Blue Skies."
8. Current events: "Joltin' Joe DiMaggio" was a popular song when the Yankee Clipper had his fifty-six-game hitting streak in 1941.

This list is far from complete. We can include other titles of songs which have become hits. (See chapter 6, "Song Topics.")

To repeat, titles come from anywhere and everywhere. Listen, read, and be attentive. When you find a good title, write it down. Keep it for future reference even if you don't "hear" a complete song immediately.[3]

---

1. I knew a chap named Johnny Boy, read of a girl named Zephyr Ann, heard of a Marine Corps private named General George Washington, lived next door to Commodore Perry Storts, and a friend is Major Parks. Rank is popular, apparently, when families want to introduce their offspring into the world with an inspiring name!

2. During my Navy tour, his girl friend asked my shipmate if we were sailing the next day. Joe answered, Texas accent and all, "Honey, if you don't believe I'm goin', just count the days I'm gone." We used that long title for a song. It was recorded by Marilyn Maye in her first album, *Marilyn. . . . The Most.*

3. I have a special file which includes some 300 titles. When time and mood prevail, they are there for me to work on.

How long should a title be? The best advice is to keep it short. There are several reasons for doing so, and with definite advantages:

1. There is less to remember when Shirley goes to the record store to buy your latest hit. It is easier for her to recall, say, "Laura," than the eight-word-title tune, "I Got It Bad and That Ain't Good."
2. You have more space in the song for your lyrical message if your title is brief.

The best reason is to study hit songs. They show the public response. While it is incorrect to state that people buy music only because of the length of the title, we can quickly observe that short-title songs predominate in hit status. Take a look at these:

One word: "Candy"; "Honey"; "Laura"; "Nola"; "Charmain"; "Diane"; "Brazil"; "Oklahoma!"; "Yesterdays"; "Home"; "Gigi"; "Stardust"; "Tenderly"; "Moonglow"; "Sylvia"; "Misty"; "Ruby"; "Dream"; "People"; "Tangerine"; "Summertime"; "If"; "Symphony"; "Mame"; "Lazybones."

Two words: "Embraceable You"; "Just You"; "Girl Talk"; "Rose Room"; "Sophisticated Lady"; "Hello, Dolly!"; "Small Hotel"; "Blue Skies"; "White Christmas"; "Blue Room"; "Easter Parade"; "My Ideal"; "Kansas City"; "Harbor Lights"; "My Romance"; "Mexicali Rose"; "Indian Summer"; "Deep Purple"; "Ev'ry Time"; "Sweet Lorraine"; "Moonlight Bay"; "Twilight Time"; "April Showers"; "Melancholy Baby"; "'Tis Autumn"; "Mairzy Doats"; "Ja-Da"; "Canadian Sunset"; "Moonlight Serenade"; "Sunrise Serenade"; "Easy Street"; "Sentimental Journey"; "Too Young."[4]

Three words: "Night and Day"; "Over the Rainbow"; "Moonlight in Vermont"; "Begin the Beguine"; "The Christmas Song"; "Stella by Starlight"; "Isle of Capri"; "My Funny Valentine"; "Tea for Two"; "Spring is Here"; "Moonlight Becomes you"; "Pennies from Heaven"; "The Trolley Song"; "Body and Soul"; "Where or When"; "Memphis in June"; "Don't Blame Me"; "I Got Rhythm"; "Memories of You"; "Fine and

---

4. "Too Young" held the record for being first the most times (twelve) on Lucky Strike's "Your Hit Parade."

Dandy"; "Time After Time"; "Love for Sale"; "Cottage for Sale"; "Chattanooga Choo-Choo"; "I Surrender, Dear"; "Did I Remember?"; "Sleepy-Time Gal"; "My Blue Heaven"; "Ol' Man River"; "Day by Day"; "I Love You"; "Little Girl Blue"; "Darktown Strutters Ball"; "Alexander's Ragtime Band"; "I'm Old-Fashioned"; "A Foggy Day."

Four words: "Sleepy-Time Down South"; "Once in a While"; "Moonlight on the Ganges"; "When Day Is Done"; "Dancing on the Ceiling"; "Dancing in the Dark"; "I Cover the Waterfront"; "Stars Fell on Alabama"; "Soon It's Gonna Rain";"Ev'rytime We Say Goodbye"; "When Sunny Gets Blue"; "Gone with the Wind"; "Thanks for the Memory"; "It's a Blue World"; "Polka-Dots and Moonbeams"; "Say It Isn't So"; "I Cried for You"; "California, Here I Come!"; "Try a Little Tenderness"; "Blues in the Night"; "The Nearness of You"; "That Old Black Magic"; "I'm Always Chasing Rainbows"; "A Tisket a Tasket"; "You are for Loving"; "How High the Moon"; "Moonlight on the Wabash"; "You'll Never Walk Alone"; "The Man I Love"; "Stairway to the Stars"; "The Night Is Young"; "I Can't Get Started."

Five words: "Rudolph the Red-Nosed Reindeer"; "You Go to My Head"; "Oh, What a Beautiful Mornin'"; "Yes, We Have No Bananas"; "Almost Like Being in Love"; "What Is There to Say?"; "Back Home Again in Indiana"; "Sunny Side of the Street"; "All the Things You Are"; "Love Is a Simple Thing"; "The Very Thought of You."

Six words: "I've Got a Crush on You"; "People Will Say We're in Love"; "June Is Bustin' Out All Over"; "Surrey with the Fringe on Top"; "How Are Things in Glocca Morra?"; "This Is the Army, Mister Jones"; "I Only Have Eyes for You"; "I've Got You Under My Skin"; "Our Love Is Here to Stay"; "Deep in the Heart of Texas."

Seven words: "I Get Along Without You Very Well"; "I Can't Give You Anything but Love"; "Praise the Lord and Pass the Ammunition"; "How Long Has This Been Going On?"; "The Best Things in Life Are Free"; "Can't Help Lovin' That Man of Mine"; "I Get a Kick Out of You."

Eight words: "Coming In on a Wing and a Prayer"; "I Got It Bad and That Ain't Good"; "On the Atchison, Topeka, and the Santa Fe"; "I've Got My Love to Keep Me Warm"; "Spring Will Be a Little Late This Year"; "You'd Be So Nice to Come Home To."

Just to illustrate a rule-proving exception, here is a *long* title: "The New Ashmoleon Marching Society and Students Conservatory Band" (*nine* words, Frank Loesser's rousing tune from his appealing 1948 score of *Where's Charlie?*).

What do these quantity-words show? They substantiate our earlier statement: Keep your title short. Here is a summary of title lengths in these 162 songs:

Number of Words	Number of Songs	Percent of Songs Considered
1	25	16
2	33	20
3	36	22
4	32	20
5	11	7
6	10	6
7	7	4
8	7	4
Many	1	1

Let successful songs point our way to successful songwriting. If 85 percent of these hits have five or fewer words in their titles, wouldn't we be wise to follow that pattern?

Another survey verifies this principle. For several years "Your Hit Parade" presented the ten most popular tunes each week. We could get involved here with how many of those first-place tunes were "repeaters" (and there were many), but we won't. Instead, note the word-quantity, or more important, the word paucity in the titles of these 332 top songs:

Number of Words	Percent of Total Songs
1	12
2	21
3	24
4	18
5	10
6	9
7	3
8	2
9	1
10	0

A summary of this title word count is:

One word	12%
Two words or less	33%
Three words or less	57%
Four words or less	75%
Five words or less	85%

These numbers reaffirm this interesting and important axiom. *Three* words in a title were the most often employed. But the critical statistic is that *85 percent* of the most popular songs during this twenty-three-year period had titles of *five words or less*. What better guideline can we follow than this record of title-word success?

Economize, word-wise, on your titles. Follow the examples of other successful songwriters: keep your titles short.

Consideration should be given to syllables. Not only is word paucity important in titles but so are syllables. For instance, "Embraceable You" is a short title. These two words have six syllables; they take up a lot of lyric space. It might as well be a six-word title. We won't split hairs on this subject, but it deserves your attention. If we aim toward minimization of title words, we should also employ brevity in their syllables.

Where do you "hang" your title? Anyplace is the answer. The best place is "up in the corner" or "at the top," as musicians say, meaning that the opening lyrics in your song are your title.

Examples: "Hello, Dolly!"; "I Cover the Waterfront"; "You Are My Sunshine"; "Love for Sale"; "I Can't Give You Anything but Love"; "I'm Always Chasing Rainbows"; "I Love You"; "Moonlight Becomes You"; "Once in a While"; "You Stepped Out of a Dream"; "Seventy-Six Trombones"; "Oklahoma!"; "Blue Skies"; "Rudolph the Red-Nosed Reindeer"; "Time After Time"; "Try to Remember."

Even if there is a "pickup" or lead-in word or two before the title, it is still a "corner" title. "Over the Rainbow"; "Small Hotel"; and "Laura" therefore qualify.

The next best title placement is at the very end of your tune. "Go out" with it, again to quote the guys on the bandstand. It leaves the listener with your title as the last thing he hears. "Body and Soul"; "Sunny Side of the Street"; "September in the Rain"; "You'll Never Walk Alone"; "My Ideal" are examples.

Songs which have titles both first and last—at the "corner" and at the end—capitalize on these advantages. Examples: "Gone with the Wind"; "Night and Day"; "Get Out of Town"; "I've Got a Crush on You"; "Sleepy-Time Gal"; "Dream"; "When Day Is Done"; "Memphis in June"; "Don't Blame Me"; "Day by Day"; "Without a Song"; "Love Is a Simple Thing"; "Dancing in the Dark"; "Spring Will Be a Little Late This Year."

To backtrack to title word-quantity, note the statistics on titles placed at both the beginning and ending of these fourteen hit songs:

Number of Words	Songs	Percent of Songs Considered
1	1	7
3	6	43
4	4	29
5	2	14
8	1	7

You can profit from both "corner" and "go out" title locations with a title of five words or less as did 93 *percent* of these songs.

Where are other titles placed if they aren't early and late? Obviously, in the middle of songs. They are in the majority. Even so, the prime location for the title is the first words heard, the next best place is the last words heard, and the optimum use of the title is both first and last.

Is there any rule which tells you where to place the title? Yes; your lyrics will help specify it. And if they don't, experiment with your lyric lines until they do.

For instance, if your title is "Then I Met You," that phrase suggests that there is introductory material, an earlier beginning, prior to stating "I met you." Your "A" phrase might read something like this:

My whole world was going wrong,
I didn't feel like singing a song;
Ev'ry day was all too long,
Then I Met You.

If your title is "I Met You," that statement lends itself to an up-in-the-corner placement, such as:

I Met You,
And that was a thrill!
Remember it I will
From now on.

This same title could also be a go-out title with this lyric story:

My world was not a happy place.
Where was my sky of blue?
All at once I saw your special face:
I Met You.

You can see that "I Met You" can be either an up-front or go-out title. Can it be both? Certainly, such as:

I Met You.
What a wonderful place my world can be
Now that I've found special company:
I Met You.

This is not to change your story. Let it speak to you. But if you can get your idea across, try to take advantage of early-and-late title positions by making changes and experimenting with it.

Throughout this book we stay with rules. Now let's look at a few exceptional rule-breaking exceptions.

Four[5] songs are unique. The titles are *never* mentioned in their lyrics. They are:

1. Mel Torme's perennial "The Christmas Song." While it is all about Christmas, it says "Christmas" only once. Yet it is a great and successful song.
2. Ralph Blane's "The Trolley Song" is a standard among standards. If the title, per se, isn't present, "trolley" is, and often.
3. "September Song" by Kurt Weill is void its title in lyrics, but "September" is frequently stated.
4. "Dancing on the Ceiling" says "dancing" twice and "ceiling" once.

If you can write the equivalent to these songs, don't bother to read further. You don't need any help!

How many times should your song mention the title in its lyrics? You can't overdo it. The rule is repeat, duplicate, ditto, and one more time.

Educators know the best way to have students retain an important point. It is not to write it, read it, put it on the chalkboard, or speak it soft/loud/slow/fast. Simply, it is to say it, then again. . .and again. . .and again. Repetition is the key. Your "important point" is stated (and some will remember), then repeated (and more will recall), then restated (and even more will retain it), and so on.

How do you recall a phone number? How do we memorize speeches? Or children learn? By this very same method of hearing it once more to the nth power. Therefore, repeat your title as often as you can.

Look at these hit songs and the frequency with which their composers stated the titles. . .

None: "The Christmas Song"; "September Song"; "Dancing on the Ceiling"; "The Trolley Song." They are great exceptions which took true composing genius to overcome this severe disadvantage.

---

5. There are others. These will illustrate the point.

One time: "All the Things You Are"[6]; "Tea for Two" +; "My Funny Valentine" + + +; "You Are for Loving." + +

Two times: "Stardust"; "Small Hotel"; "My Ideal"; "April Showers"; "Embraceable You" +; "Time After Time"; "Fine and Dandy"; "How High the Moon"; "White Christmas" +; "Rudolph the Red-Nosed Reindeer." + + + + +

Three times: "Stars Fell on Alabama"; "What Is There to Say?"; "Moonlight Becomes You"; "This Is the Army, Mister Jones"; "Easter Parade"; "Polka-Dots and Moonbeams"; "People Will Say We're in Love"; "Body and Soul"; "Where or When"; "How Long Has This Been Going On?"; "My Blue Heaven"; "I've Got a Crush on You"; "Pennies from Heaven"; "Me and My Shadow"; "Over the Rainbow" +; "I'm Always Chasing Rainbows"; "Thanks for the Memory"; "Little Girl Blue." +

Four times: "Gone with the Wind" + + + +; "Moonlight in Vermont"; "Oh, What a Beautiful Mornin'" + +; "Memphis in June"; "My Romance"; "Chattanooga Choo-Choo" + +; "Too Young."

Five times: "Night and Day" +; "Don't Blame Me" + + + + +; "Day by Day"; "Tenderly."

Six times: "Ol' Man River"; "Blue Skies."

Seven times: "Ev'ry Time"; "Soon It's Gonna Rain." +

More: "Candy" (eight times).

There is a reason for the + by some of these titles. How do you count the lyric phrase "day and night" in "Night and Day"? It isn't an exact repeat, and yet the words are identical, if inverted. It deserves something short of a full repeat credit. Mark it + because it serves the same purpose; it helps us retain the song title when we hear it.

Look at the last line in "White Christmas." It has the same words in different order. Give it a + on the tally sheet.

---

6. "All the Things You Are," the Hammerstein-Kern classic, was the sole perennial from the 1939 unsuccessful musical *Very Warm for May*. Its title appears only in the final four bars. By rights, "You Are" should be its title since those two words appear four times.

"Gone with the Wind" is stated four times, and the word "gone" is also used four times, for a score of 4 + + + +.

"Tea for Two" is used, amazingly, only once in Irving Caesar's great standard. The phrase "two for tea" rates a definite +.

"Don't Blame Me" has its title five times, and the word "blame" five more times for a final tally of 5 + + + + +.

Only once is the title mentioned in "My Funny Valentine," but "valentine" is repeated thrice to give it a 1 + + +.

"Chattanooga Choo-Choo" appears three times; "Chattanooga" and "choo-choo" are mentioned additionally once each. A four-bar tag (here is a fine example of what a tag can do for your song. See chapter 17: "The Tag Ending") again gives the full title plus another "choo-choo." Its ultimate score is 4 + + + +.

"Rudolph the Red-Nosed Reindeer" says its title twice, mentions "reindeer" thrice, and "Rudolph" two more times. It merits a score of 2 + + + + +.

"You Are for Loving" is said only once, then states "loving" two more times. Total: 1 + +.[7]

While we urge the + factor for parts of title repetition, we considered only those fifty-one songs with full-title repeats in the following statistics. They are important to recognize:

Times Title Stated	Number of Songs	Percent of Songs Considered
0	3	6[8]
1	4	8
2	10	20
3	18	35
4	7	13
5	4	8
6	2	4
7	2	4
8	1	2

---

7. I first heard this song in 1960 at Kansas City's Starlight Theatre. My guest was Tandy Craig, assistant musical director of the Tennessee Ernie Ford Show, as we saw *Meet Me in St. Louis*. The song ended, and we looked at each other as if to say, "Wow! Why haven't we heard that great song before?" Maybe we hadn't because it didn't follow this basic repeat-the-title rule.

8. We repeat that these songs are highly exceptional.

Note that two, three, and four times the title is mentioned predominate, totaling 68 percent of the songs considered.

The point is fundamental, simple, and clear. Repeat your title often, or part of it if the entire title won't fit. Give credit to a title word which carries the same meaning. Remember: repetition demands retention—by the listener.

Do *not* mention your title in the bridge. As stated in chapter 15 ("The Bridge"), the requirement of a bridge is to contrast with the "A" phrase, both musically and lyrically. Yes, this rule has been violated; but the best structured songs have no title in that "B" phrase.

Are there any guidelines regarding specific words to use in a title? We studied the 332 first-place songs of "Your Hit Parade" survey. That analysis provided several important observations.

Words employed in titles range, by grammatical definition, from adjectives through verbs. There are words commencing on every letter of the alphabet except Q, X, and Z. It won't surprise you to learn that they include proper names, cities, states, months, seasons, weather, celestial conditions, flowers, days, and foreign words, to name only a few.

Specifically they included *autumn, Broadway, coins, daddy, eyes, fools, gypsy, hill, imagination, journey, kisses, lagoon, melody, nothing, orchids, partners, rumors, sin, time, unchained, vaya, walk,* and *yellow.*

We found *kind, kiss, kisses, kissing, knew,* and *know* under "K". Words starting with "Y" included *years, yellow, you, you'll, young,* and *you're.*

There are 588 different title words used in those 332 top songs. They ranged from *a* through *yours.* They addressed a host of subjects—nearly "everything under the sun and moon," including those words.

Used only once in all of those 332 songs were 436 different words. Words repeated in many titles numbered 152. The most popular, judging from their appearances in different songs, were these (the paranthetical numbers show their frequency):

the	(59)	my	(20)
you	(40)	to	(14)
a	(33)	and	(11)
I	(28)	me	(11)
love	(28)	heart	(10)
in	(27)	all	(10)
of	(24)	song	(9)

From this study, we can draw these apparent conclusions regarding title words:

1. The majority of the most-repeated words are not germane to the title's subject (such as *the*, *a*, *in*, *of*, etc.).
2. Of the two important pronouns, *you* appears more often than *I* (40 as against 28).
3. *Love* (which is both a verb and a noun), *heart*, and *song* are significant; they were present 28, 10, and 9 times.
4. Most song titles are love-oriented. Even if their titles don't specifically address it, love is the central theme in them.
5. Of other-than-love subjects, titles run the same broad topical span you will find in chapter 6. Some examples include "White Christmas"; "The Woodpecker Song"; "Sixteen Tons"; "Nature Boy"; "Deep in the Heart of Texas"; "Pennies from Heaven"; "Accentuate the Positive"; "Elmer's Tune"; "Mairzy Doats"; "Mule Train."

With these few exceptions mentioned, there are no dominant reappearing words in song titles. We see that a considerable number of them have been and can be used. We are relatively unrestricted in the use of words in our title.

How "honest" are song titles? Do they sing about what the title says? Do they specifically relate to the subject? Or are they a lost leader, getting our attention and then trekking off on the musical staff into a lyrical night of unadvertised territory?

Most song titles don't kid us. "Deep in the Heart of Texas" explains happy conditions in the Lone Star State. "White Christmas" is sure-enough about a white Christmas. "Rudolph the Red-Nosed Reindeer" praises that Yule hero.

In love songs, many are equally honest. Examples include "I'm in the Mood for love"; "All My Love"; "People Will Say We're in Love"; "You and I"; "Tonight We Love."

Yet many are not. Some non-love-sounding titles are often love-oriented. For instance:

"Chattanooga Choo-Choo" may lead us to think that it is about a train—and it is. However, its final phrase takes the singer back home aboard that train to his waiting girl.

"Don't Sit Under the Apple Tree" has little to do with either sitting or the orchard stock. It is a love message. The gist of its gist is that she must refrain from doing so, except with the singer.

"A Bushel and a Peck" isn't a marketplace quantity. Instead, it is a poetic measurement of how much the singer loves someone.

"Surrey with the Fringe on Top" brags about this fancy mode of transportation, but that vehicle is important only because it carries a young couple in love.

"It Might as Well Be Spring" is not only non-seasonal; it explains the disoriented condition which love has produced in the singer.

Other not-very-honest but excellent titles of appealing songs include "East of the Sun"; "A Foggy Day"; "What Is There to Say?"; "Night and Day"; "The Gypsy."

Love song titles which specifically relate to their messages can be positive, negative, and in-between "maybe/if." There is no mistaking the point of view which each expresses.

Examples of positive songs, which their titles clearly indicate, are "I Love You"; "I'm Yours"; "You're a Sweetheart"; "My Darling, My Darling"; "You Go to My Head"; "It Had to Be You"; "So in Love"; "You're Mine."

The middle ground of the uncertain is just that: somewhat indefinite, perhaps possible, and hopeful. Examples include "If I Give My Love to You"; "If I Loved You"; "I Wish I Knew."

Most negative titles follow with an honest and not-very-happy message. Examples include "Alone"; "It's a Blue World"; "You're Breaking My Heart"; "Gone with the Wind"; "A Ghost of a Chance"; "I Can't Get Started"; "Cottage for Sale."

Employ titles which are succinctly to the point of what your song sings. Use titles which hint at but are less closely associated with the subject and content of your song. Both work for public following, appreciation, and acceptance.

Our survey inquiry sent to some 150 people contains several interesting comments regarding titles. These are worth your attention:

1. "The Christmas Song" was listed as "Chestnuts Roasting by an Open Fire." Those six words are the opening lyrics of this magnificent song.
2. "Que Será Será" was listed as "Whatever Will Be Will Be." Might that be due to lack of recognition of this Spanish title?
3. "You'll Never Walk Alone" was listed as "When You Walk Through a Storm." As is the case of "The Christmas Song," these opening lyrics were thought to be its title. "You'll Never Walk Alone" appears twice at the end of the song, the second time as a tag (which was a familiar habit of Rodgers and Hammerstein and again illustrates the value of a title-appearing tag).

Are titles which ask a question worth our study? Yes, although they are few in number. Of these 162 songs, only three of them appear: "Did I Remember?"; "What Is There To Say?"; and "How Are Things in Glocca Morra?" That is a scant percentage of the total. There are many others, however: "How Long Has This Been Going On?"; "Do I Love You Because You're Beautiful?"; "Will You Still Be Mine?"; "Remember Me?"; "Are You Lonesome Tonight?"; "Did You Ever See a Dream Walking?"

These "question" titles are in the minority. But they are a valid convention and have achieved hit status. Use this approach, knowing that you have good company in your "question-mark" song.

Every field of commercial endeavor recognizes the importance of a title. Many businesses use quick-identification names for the same purpose as we songwriters do: to draw attention to our firm/product by means of a unique name. Note these attention-getting titles for these non-musical businesses: "Wear Else Fashions," "Junque, Inc.," "That Type of Stuff," "Cap'n Kidd Travel," "Joantiques," "Etcetera," and "The Patchwork Closet."

Surely the ultimate value of a title is to have it become a generic term. Its trademarked name represents the entire scope of competing products and not just a single brand. They are few in popular usage, but they have meant millions of dollars to their manufacturers because of the standout popularity of that item.

The only true generic term in our musical world is one song. If someone says, "Let's sing happy birthday to good ol' Rick," the assembled throng doesn't have to search its collective mind to see which birthday tune it will sing: the song is "Happy Birthday."

If you write a song which becomes a generic term, you won't have to go to the bank; you'll own it!

We recognize how vital titles are in selling any product, be it a song, a car, or a soft drink. Apparently it is of less importance for a stage production. For instance, what does the title of Tennessee Williams' dramatic classic, *Cat on a Hot Tin Roof*, tell you about this play? Is it about a cat, or a hot tin roof? Neither. Nor do *The Rose Tattoo*, *Streetcar Named Desire*, and *Toys in the Attic* concern the subject of those great dramas. Neither do *The Iceman Cometh*, *Ah, Wilderness*, and *The Time of Your Life*.

Other straight plays relate to their titles: *Our Town*, *Life with Father*, *Tobacco Road*, *The Diary of Anne Frank*, *The Great Sebastians*, *Dial M for Murder*, *Watch on the River Rhine*, and *Romanoff and Juliet*.

The musical stage more closely—but not always—associates its titles to the story presented to the audience. *The King and I* is about a king. *Hello, Dolly!* concerns Dolly. *My Fair Lady* centers around her. *Mame* is about Mame. *Fiorello!* leaves no doubt as to its primary character. *1776* is America declaring independence. Some others are less explicit: *Best Foot Forward*, *Pipe Dreams*, *Paint Your Wagon*, *The Fantastiks*.

All of these plays/musicals have enjoyed immense success. That their titles were successful names attached to great stage productions is without doubt. Let us pose the question: Might titles which were related to the subject matter have added to further success for these plays?

You decide. Those not-to-the-subject titles may work well in many instances on the stage, but do not divorce yourself from the importance of a title and its repetition in your songs.

We have discussed titles at length. We have gone outside the musical field to show their commercial importance. We cannot overstress their value, be it to a song, a product, or a business.

We recall them all because of their names. The same is true of the music-buying public. They don't ask for a record of "a slow, danceable tune" or a "a holiday song"; they specifically want to buy "Stardust" or "White Christmas."

In summary, we find these truths to be self-evident:

1. Get a good, catchy, appealing title.
2. Keep it short—five words or less.
3. Say it often, at least three times.
4. Mention the title words in different order, or state part of it, which counts for a +.
5. The best place for the title is at the very beginning.
6. The next best place for it is at the end.
7. The optimum title placement is both "up in the corner" and "go out" with it.

Follow in the steps of those who have found success, and your title parallels the advantages employed by our famous mentors. If you do, your title will help your song become a hit in every way that can be expected of it.[9]

These items have absolutely nothing to do with the musical subject at hand but are mentioned here for a chuckle:

There is an old saw as to whether it is a preacher's special hymn entitled "Gladly the Cross I'd Bear" or is the name of the zookeeper's favorite animal, "Gladly, the Cross-Eyed Bear."

---

9. I recently wrote a song entitled "Jane!" It follows every rule: AABA, thirty-two bars and a four-bar tag, 9th range, written in the key of C, has eighty-five words. Now look at this: the title is stated thirty-seven times, or 43.5 percent of all lyrics are its single title word. Therefore, I claim the title-repeating championship! It has not been offered for publication. I'm glad to report that Jane, for whom it was written, was thrilled!

A book written by Ring Lardner in 1962 has a great title: *Shut Up, He Explained.*

That information is provided at no extra charge as is this friendly advice: Repeat your title, repeat your title, repeat your title!

C. HERE ARE TODAY'S MUSICAL HEADLINES!

CHAPTER SIX

SONG TOPICS
or What Is Your Musical Story About?

What are lyrics? That gets an easy answer—the words of a song.

Where do they come from? That also is easy—out of your vivid and creative imagination.

Now we get into a more difficult question: How do I know that what is floating through my head will make good lyrics? That answer is tough; nobody knows.

There are a few landmarks. The best is to analyze the characteristics of those songs which have lived through the years and put our material into a similar framework.

We can write about nearly any subject and set it to music. Songwriters have done so; songwriters still do. There are twenty-two different topics of lyric writing stated here. They have been popular. Most remain so today. Note these categories and their examples . . .

1. *Girls' Names:* "Diane"; "Charmain"; "Nancy with the Laughing Face"; "When Sunny Gets Blue"; "Rosemarie"; "Good Night, Irene"; "Candy"; "Sylvia"; "Once in Love with Amy"; "Nola"; "Ruby."

2. *Men's Names:* "Oh, Johnny, Oh!"; "Jim"; "Happiness Is Just a Thing Called Joe"; "Joey, Joey, Joey."

Maybe we should also include these "he" titles: "Mister Touchdown"; "When I Marry Mister Snow"; "Mister Wonderful"; "This Is the Army, Mister Jones"; "The Gentleman Is a Dope."

3. *Geography:* This can be further broken down into subcategories.

   a. *States:* "Tennessee Waltz"; "Oklahoma!"; "Moonlight in Vermont"; "Poor Little Rhode Island"; "Stars Fell on Alabama"; "Connecticut"; "Missouri Waltz"; "Maryland, My Maryland"; "Georgia on My Mind"; "Just a Little Bit South of North Carolina"; "I Want to Go Back to West Virginia."

   b. *Cities:* "Memphis in June"; "I Left My Heart in San Francisco"; "Moon over Miami"; "April in Paris"; "St. Louis Blues"; "Chicago"; "Wonderful Copenhagen"; "On a Little Street in Singapore"; "Chattanooga Choo-Choo"; "Kalamazoo"; "Albuquerque"; "Managua, Nicaragua"; "Ev'rything's Up to Date in Kansas City."

   c. *Places/Regions:* "Moonlight on the Ganges"; "Springtime in the Rockies"; "In Ol' Cape Cod"; "The Isle of Capri."

4. *Home:* "Cottage for Sale"; "Home on the Range"; "Home"; "Love in a Home"; "Bless This House."

5. *Weather:* "April Showers"; "Soon It's Gonna Rain"; "Stormy Weather"; "September in the Rain"; "Got My Love to Keep Me Warm"; "A Foggy Day"; "Gone with the Wind"; "Misty"; "Over the Rainbow"; "I'm Always Chasing Rainbows"; "Lilacs in the Rain"; "Right as the Rain"; "Singin' in the Rain."

6. *Seasons:* "Summertime"; "Spring Will Be a Little Late This Year"; "Spring Is Here"; "It Might as Well Be Spring"; "Indian Summer"; "Early Autumn"; "Spring Can Really Hang You Up the Most"; "Autumn in New York"; "Winter Wonderland."

7. *Months:* "April in Paris"; "April Showers"; "I'll Remember April"; "September Song"; "September in the Rain"; "June Is Bustin' Out All Over."

8. *Patriotic:* "God Bless America," every song about our country, the five military service songs, and the score of *This Is the Army.*[1]

   This song topic is prevalent during wartime. There were many great songs about patriotism and service life during World War II. That was our last war "with banners and songs" as the journalists state. Here are some of them which

---

1. Irving Berlin wrote this military musical with all its all-service cast. At the National Theatre in Washington in 1943, I saw Mr. Berlin perform. As the curtain opened he was sleeping on an Army cot; he yawned and in his World War I uniform got up to sing "Oh, How I Hate to Get Up in the Morning." That was a thrill I well recall.

added to our national spirit: "Praise the Lord and Pass the Ammunition"; "The White Cliffs of Dover"; "In My Arms"; "Coming In on a Wing and a Prayer"; "What Do You Do in the Infantry?"; "We're the Seabees of the Navy"; "Johnny Doughboy Found a Rose in Ireland"; "I Left My Heart at a Stage-Door Canteen."

The only military tune achieving popularity since that time was "The Ballad of the Green Berets" published in 1966. With our world at peace, may the war song depart and may we have no more need for it.

9. *Football/College fight songs:* "Mister Touchdown." Probably the best known are those of the universities of Wisconsin, Illinois, Michigan, Cornell, Indiana, Notre Dame, Minnesota, Texas, Oklahoma, Georgia Tech, and California.[2]

10. *Dream:* "I Had the Craziest Dream"; "I Dream of You"; "Dream"; "Dream a Little Dream of Me"; "You Stepped Out of a Dream"; "I Found a Dream"; "All I Have to Do Is Dream"; "I Can Dream, Can't I?"; "I'll Buy That Dream"; "Deep in a Dream"; "Darn That Dream"; "Day Dream"; "When My Dreamboat Comes Home"; "You Can't Stop Me from Dreaming"; "My Dreams Are Getting Better All the Time."

11. *Celestial:* "Stardust"; "Polka-Dots and Moonbeams"; "Twilight Time"; "Moonlight on the Ganges"; "Moonlight on the Wabash"; "Pennies from Heaven"; "Moonlight Bay"; "Stars Fell on Alabama"; "Moonlight in Vermont"; "Canadian Sunset"; "Moonlight Becomes You"; "Moon over Miami"; "Deep Purple"; "Moonlight Serenade"; "Sunrise Serenade"; "Moonglow"; "Sunrise, Sunset"; "Blue Skies"; "I Got the Sun in the Morning"; "Stairway to the Stars"; "How High the Moon"; "That Ol' Devil Moon"; "The Moon Is Yellow"; "East of the Sun"; "Ole Buttermilk Sky"; "Red Sails in the Sunset."

---

2. A friend commented that if he were to write a college fight song, his subjects would be "Hit a Home Run"; "Shoot a Free Throw"; "Hurdle Those Hurdles"; "Pull on Your Oars"; "Blast That Serve"; "A Hole in One"; and "Starboard Tack." He recognized that many college songs are football-oriented, and that there was no competition in these other sports/song areas; there has never been a popular fight song for baseball, basketball, track, crew, tennis, golf, or sailing.

12. *Train:* With the decrease of our trains, this topic is no longer as important as it was a generation ago. Perhaps it is as passe as a song about a horse and buggy might be. However, railroads have provided rhythmic, adventurous, and dramatic romance on the American scene.

If "Amtrak" lacks that flavor, look at the sound and sight and color of trains which inspired our songwriters to produce these great songs: "Atchison, Topeka, and the Santa Fe"; "Casey Jones"; "Chattanooga Choo-Choo"; "Wabash Cannonball"; "I Took a Trip on a Train"; "Blues in the Night"; "Take the A Train"; "Sentimental Journey."

13. *Night/Day:* "Yesterdays"; "Night and Day"; "Day by Day"; "The Night Is Young"; "You and the Night and the Music"; "Blues in the Night"; "When Day Is Done"; "Daybreak"; "A Foggy Day."

14. *Marches:* "Seventy-Six Trombones"; "The New Ashmoleon Marching Society and Students Conservatory Band"; "Buckle Down, Winsocki."

15. *Foreign words:*
German - "Dankeschein"; "Auf Wiederseh'n, Sweetheart."
Spanish - "Amapola"; "Amor"; "Que Sera Sera"; "Besame Mucho"; "Perdido"; "Vaya Con Dios"; "Frenesi."
French - "Mam'selle"; "C'Est Moi."
Yiddish - "Bie Mir Bist Du Schoen."
Swedish - "The Hut Sut Song."
Belgian - "Dominique."
Italian - "Volare."

16. *Fraternity/Sorority:* Only one tune in this category has ever met with commercial success and public applause— "The Sweetheart of Sigma Chi."

17. *Taken from the classics:* This area is as much melodic as it is lyrical. These musical airs are in the public domain. They have been adapted with modern lyrics and have found popular acclaim. That none of them have been recent favorites may tell us something about their current appeal in the musical market. However, this musical category was once important and might be worth your consideration. The list is impressive:

Song	Original Classic	Words/Music Adapters	Year
"I'm Always Chasing Rainbows"	Chopin theme	Joseph McCarthy and Harry Carroll	1918
"Tonight We Love"	First movement of Tchaikovsky's First Piano Concerto (The famous recording by the Freddy Martin Band was surely important for its success.)	Worth, Austin, and Freddy Martin	1941
"Till the End of Time"	Chopin's Polonaise in A flat	Buddy Kaye and Ted Mossman	1945
"Full Moon and Empty Arms"	Rachmaninoff's Piano Concerto Number Two	Buddy Kaye and Ted Mossman	1946
Score from the musical stage play *Kismet*	Borodin's Themes	Robert Wright and George Forrest	1953

18. *Philosophical:* If ever a message was didactically set to music, it was through this category. These familiar examples provide inspirational encouragement:[3] "Climb Every Mountain"; "The Impossible Dream"; "If"; "You'll Never Walk Alone."

19. *Flowers:* "My Violet"; "Honeysuckle Rose"; "I'll Buy You Violets for Your Fur"; "Ramblin' Rose"; "Red Roses for a Blue Lady"; "Give Me One Dozen Roses"; "Rose of San Antone"; "Roses of Piccardy."

20. *Walk:* "Let's Take an Old-Fashioned Walk"; "You Walked by"; "I'll Walk Alone"; "Did You Ever See a Dream Walking?"; "You'll Never Walk Alone"; "Walking My Baby Back Home"; "I Don't Want to Walk Without You, Baby"; "I'm Walking Behind You."

21. *Heart:* "Heart and Soul"; "This Heart of Mine"; "My Heart Tells Me"; "My Foolish Heart"; "Here Is My Heart"; "Says My Heart"; "You're Breaking My Heart."

22. *Love:* Probably every other song written is about love, an always-fresh subject which finds a place on the charts, in our acclaim, and in the songwriting market. This topic needs to be considered in these approaches, since love takes one of two routes:

    a. I love her and she loves me, and we will live happily ever after, or

    b. I love her but she doesn't love me, so here is my lament.

    They are either positive or negative in lyric message. Consider these examples:

    Positive: "Thou Swell, Thou Pretty"; "My Funny Valentine"; "I Surrender, Dear"; "You Stepped Out of a Dream"; "How Long Has This Been Going On?"; "I Love You!"; "I've Got a Crush on You"; "Our Love Is Here to Stay"; "Katy"; "Redwing"; "What Is There to Say?"; "The Very Thought of You"; "Polka-Dots and Moonbeams";

---

3. An exception which doesn't is "Ol' Man River." It is a negative narrative of the troubles, problems, and hard work of a man.

"Night and Day"; "Day by Day"; "I Can't Give You Anything but Love"; "I Get a Kick Out of You"; "The Nearness of You"; "I'll Take Romance."

Negative: "Cottage for Sale"; "Gone with the Wind"; "A Ghost of a Chance"; "These Foolish Things"; "Once in a While"; "Everything Happens to Me"; "Spring Is Here"; "I Can't Get Started with You"; "Thanks for the Memory"; "It's a Blue World"; "I Cover the Waterfront"; "Little Girl Blue"; "Spring Will Be a Little Late This Year"; "There's No You."

Of the thirty-four songs listed under the "love" category, twenty are positive and fourteen are negative in their lyrical messages. Apparently the apreciative public favors the happy story set to music, but only slightly—59 percent to 41 percent. About six out of every ten love songs have an affirmative/positive approach.

Another discipline under the "love" category should be considered.

Do your lyrics speak of "my girl" or "that girl" or "you, girl!"? If so, they are *specific* in their approach.

Or do they refer to "a girl," "some girl," or "any girl"? Then you have written in a *general* framework.

To fall under the *specific* category, a song need not be so definite as to state "Ruth, I love you," but it must be directed toward a precise and unmistakable someone. A "you" isn't every girl you pass on the street; it is a specific girl, almost as if she were mentioned by name.

Look at these *specific* examples: "Embraceable You"; "Small Hotel"; "Polka-Dots and Moonbeams"; "Moonlight Becomes You"; "Night and Day"; "All the Things You Are"; "Too Young." Each relates to a definite "you," and not just anybody.

Of course, the ultimate in *specific* lyrics spells out just one person. Examples are "Bill"; "Mister Touchdown"; "Once in Love with Amy"; "Candy"; "Nancy with the Laughing Face"; and all other proper names.

In contrast, *general* means just that: it isn't specific. Study the lyrics of "My Ideal"; "The Girl That I Marry"; and "They Say It's Wonderful." You will see that they sing about love without relating to a particular person or some special "you."

These topics have been fertile ground in pop music during the past half century. It seems an odds-on bet that the vast majority of them will remain popular in American songs, because they center around vital things in our lives.

Don't be limited to these topics alone, but you can feel safe if they are your subject matter.

CHAPTER SEVEN

HOLIDAY, CALENDAR, SEASONAL, AND SPECIAL EVENTS SONGS
or They Bloom Every Year!

These song types deserve special mention and your special attention. They have rules, benefits, and drawbacks all their own which apply to no other songs. To some degree, special event and seasonal songs share the same characteristics, but neither is quite so pronounced in both limiting factors and advantages as are holiday songs. Specific traits are (1) they have a short market time, and (2) if they hit, they "bloom" every year.

When we try to sell a song about love, that subject is always popular. We have the entire year in which to market it. Regardless of whether it is negative or positive, win or lose, those love conditions are continually in season. Love songs find listeners who share their emotions every day.

Such is not the case with holiday songs. A Christmas tune has from Thanksgiving night through December 25, a time span of about thirty days, in which to capture the public's fancy. The activity required by a music producer to put your song (and his investment) in the black is intense. He faces a large capital outlay with a short time frame to blitz the market and break into the charts, which are now occupied by about fifteen Christmas standards.

A longtime friend was courteous but adamantly negative when I approached him with Christmas and Easter songs. (He is a songwriter himself and general manager of a record company.) He told me they take no chances on holiday and special events songs. The investment risk is too great on a short-term promotion. They stay with the current material which has a year-long appeal. He went on to say that "maybe they miss some things." What record firm wouldn't like to have another "Rudolph"? But he said they play for the rest of the year and give Christmas to somebody else.

Before you become discouraged with that answer, remember: If your song hits, it will probably "bloom" every year. Look at the success which Johnny Marks' "Rudolph the Red-Nosed Reindeer"[1] and Mel Torme's "The Christmas Song" have enjoyed. Add to them "I'll Be Home for Christmas"; "All I Want for Christmas Is My Two Front Teeth"; "I Saw Mama Kissing Santa Claus"; "I Heard the Bells on Christmas Day"; "Have Yourself a Merry Little Christmas"; "White Christmas"; "We Need a Little Christmas" (from the stage hit *Mame*), plus the church hymns and the winter songs of "Jingle Bells"; "I've Got My Love to Keep Me Warm"; "Frosty the Snowman"; "Baby, It's Cold Outside"; "Let It Snow"; and "Winter Wonderland." We hear them every season. And every year the record companies, recording artists, and songwriters trudge through the snow with a very warm feeling en route to the bank!

Surely the Christmas musical market is crowded. But keep in mind that, except for the sacred songs, many of them are relative newcomers. Irving Berlin's "White Christmas" joined us in 1942, and both "The Christmas Song" and "Rudolph" made our Christmas merrier circa 1946 and 1949 respectively.

Is there room for another Christmas song? Absolutely—yours! Write it, market it, and join "Rudolph." Let us enjoy it when you headline the Christmas musical season next year.

If your Yuletide is full of music, the rest of the holiday market has scarcely been touched.

Who owns Easter—at least musically? Irving Berlin, of course, with his "Easter Parade." (That illustrious composer wrote

---

1. The legend regarding "Rudolph" is interesting. Marks offered it to several artists, including Dinah Shore and Bing Crosby. He approached Gene Autry who was lukewarm toward "Rudolph," but Gene's wife liked the song and he recorded it for her. That was 150 million records ago. The rest is a triumphant history in virtually every language. Marks has made millions from this great song—and not from the song alone. "Rudolph" has branched out into books, wearing apparel, and stuffed animals, all of which produce a royalty for its songwriter.

this song for a play. It was entitled "Show Your Little Dimple" but not used. You can see that its title contains the same six syllables as the first line of "Easter Parade." It was easily changed with new lyrics to this classic as we know it.) "Here Comes Peter Cottontail" shares the Easter stage, but to a far lesser degree.

Easter has room for and needs your tunes. Look at that "bloom annually" market and be a part of it.

That covers our two big religious holidays. What about the New Year? Its only popular song is "What Are You Doing New Year's Eve?" The limited market time will draw a "no thank you" from many producers; they have only a week from Christmas through January 1 to impress the public with your song. However, there is a musical void for that celebrated holiday, and it well deserves your attention.

There has never been a popular Jewish holiday song. The Jewish New Year is in late September. Yom Kippur occurs about the first of October. Hanukkah is approximately a week before Christmas. Passover is around Easter. There are other holidays important to members of the Jewish faith. With the lack of musical competition, this area might be worthy of your talents.

Study our other holidays. Independence Day has all of the great patriotic American songs. What about Mother's Day, Father's Day, Memorial Day, Armistice Day, Labor Day? At Thanksgiving its songs are church hymns. We have hymns at Christmas and Easter, but we also hear non-religious numbers then. Shouldn't the same be true at Thanksgiving? This is fertile ground to put a songwriter annually on the charts.

Let's go a step further: How about a birthday tribute to Lincoln or Washington, an ode (in a minor key?) to Hallowe'en, and a salute to Arbor Day and Veterans Day?

Carry this idea an additional step. Few states, cities, and places have musical trademarks (see chapter 6, "Song Topics"). That leaves a lot of territory needing songs.

Or the anniversary of the repeal of prohibition, or Teddy Roosevelt's San Juan Hill victory, or Groundhog's Day, or Vote on Election Day. Want some titles? "Gin Is In"; "Good Ol'

Teddy"; "How's Your Shadow?". ("I Like Ike," a political tribute, came out of *Call Me Madame* in 1950.)

Esquire's *Handbook for Hosts*, on page 266, lists "365 excuses for a party." They range from "Happy hangover day" on January 1, through December 31 with the anniversary of the National Football Coaches Association luncheon. It might be worth studying.

What about a song for February 29? That once-in-four-years-day is unique. It should be easy for an imaginative songwriter to put Leap Year in music.

Ridiculous? Maybe. But a lot of hit songs have a lot flimsier basis than these ideas.

February 14 belongs to Rodgers and Hart. "My Funny Valentine" is the only well-known tune for that dedicated-to-lovers day. There is plenty of market time following Christmas to establish a new song.

Look at the seasonal songs which celebrate events month by month, and have musical fun with a particular time of year:

January - The winter songs, most of which we are tired of because they have been overplayed at Christmas.

February - "My Funny Valentine."

March - None.

April - "I'll Remember April"; "April in Paris"; "April Showers."

May - None.

June - "June Is Bustin' Out All Over"; "Memphis in June."

July - The patriotic songs of Independence Day.

August - None.

September - "September Song"; "September in the Rain."

October - None.

November - Martin and Blane wrote "Thanksgiving" for Doris Day, but it was never published.

December - The many Christmas songs we know.

Consider those wide open spaces on the calendar calling for you to write a hit song where none exist now.

Here is a musical visit through the seasons:

Winter - Cold weather songs stated earlier.

Spring - "It Might as Well Be Spring"; "Spring Can Really Hang You Up the Most"; "Springtime in the Rockies."

Summer - "In the Good Old Summertime."

Autumn - "Indian Summer"; "Autumn in New York."

Some of the songs mentioned under the "month" listing apply here. But there is plenty of room for your song to be heard and sung every season.[1]

Navigate your own musical course through the year. Here is a calendar of topics about which you might write.

---

1. I wrote a theatrical revue, *Stamp Out the New Year*. It had a song, and sometimes several, for each month. The idea was to get away from the stereotyped activity and point up a little-known event. Some of them may seem incredible to you. But remember that we songwriters are always looking for ways to address every entertaining subject with a fresh approach. Take a look at my departure from the norm:

Month Skit	Song Title
January	"Resolutions!"
February	"Groundhog"
March	"I've Given You Up for Lent"
April	"Income Tax Time"
May	"The PTA Meeting"
June	"There Goes My Little Girl" (marriage)
July	"My Good Old Independence Days"
August	"Don't Ever Take a Vacation!"
September	"Fight, You Green and Gold Grasshoppers!" (baseball)
October	"You're My Favorite Witch"
November	"Wait Till Next Year" (a losing football team)
December	"I Don't Want to Be Santa Claus"

Season	Month	Holiday	Activities	Weather
Winter	January	New Year's Eve/Day	Bowl Games Superbowl Resolutions	Cold
	February	Lincoln/Washington/Valentine	Winter sports Ground Hog Day	
	March	St. Patrick's/Easter		
		. . . .		
Spring	April	Easter	Baseball season starts Income tax time	Warm
	May	Mother's Day/Memorial Day	Flowers blooming Picnics Stanley Cup Indy 500 Kentucky Derby Spring activities Gardening Warm weather sports	

Season	Month	Holiday	Activities	Weather
	June	Father's Day/Flag Day	Weddings School out Graduation	Hot
		. . . .		
Summer	July	Independence Day	Summer activities	
	August	None (state and local?)	Vacations	
	September	Labor Day	Back to school Football season starts	
		. . . .		
Autumn	October	Columbus Day/Veterans Day/ Hallowe'en	Fall activities World Series Trick or treat	Cool
	November	Thanksgiving	Elections	
	December	Christmas	Holiday parties	
		. . . .		

There are many events which have never been saluted in song. They are truly special occurrences which happen to most of us during our lifetimes. Here are some possibilities which might strike your composing fancy:

Event	Possible Titles
Birthday	"You Can't Be Twenty-One!"
A trip abroad	"We're Going to France"
Housewarming	"Come and Be Welcome"
Birth of a child	"Hoorah for Your New Baby!"
Purchase of a new car	"You're Riding in Style!"
A victory	"Salute the Winner!"
A reunion	"Old Friends, Dear Friends"
An honor	"Congratulations, Mister President!"

Whatever the season, month, holiday, activity, and weather, there is tuneful territory for your song to commemorate. Employ your talented time as your muse directs. Much of this domain is musically virgin country. Its specific limitations are understandable; the possibilities of annual returns provide real incentives to the market-ambitious songwriter.

"White Christmas" found "room at the inn." We hope that your song will, too.

CHAPTER EIGHT

NOVELTY SONGS
or Why Didn't I Think of That Nutty Idea?

This is a unique type of song. Its lyrics are usually nonsensical. It is based on an offbeat idea, which is what makes it a novelty song.

The last of these nonconforming hits was a top-chart item about 1943. Because of its long absence from popular acclaim, perhaps a market for it no longer exists. But that does not mean that it might not reoccur through your innovative talent.

Let's take a look at these examples which found public fancy for thirty years.

"Ja-Da" captured the musical hearts of the "flapper" era when it appeared in 1918. This Bob Carleton lively number has lyrics which are strictly "chant" syllables until it gets into conventional words at the bridge of this AABA tune. "Ja-Da" has stood the test of time and remains as a jazz and musicians' favorite.

In 1936 "The Music Goes Round and Round" was musically contagious. A singer on stage made it visibly attractive, as if he were playing a tuba, and the music went "round and round" before he made it finally emerge—with gestures—from that instrument to the joy of his audience.

A band leader made "Ti-Pi-Tin" famous after earlier rejections. This Maria Grever tune had original Spanish lyrics. English words were provided by Raymond Leveen, and everybody sang, whistled, and danced to it in 1938.

In 1939 "Three Little Fishes" was a big seller. Its popular recordings had the public enjoying its baby-talk lyrics.

"The Woodpecker Song" was hot musical news in 1940. If you don't recall it, you can well imagine that it had a series of eighth and sixteenth notes in a woodpecker-pecking-on-wood staccato effect.

"The Hut Sut Song" followed in 1941. This upbeat number had a "cheerleader" sound with phonetics which Americans had never heard before. They might as well have been Greek to us, but they weren't. Those uncommon syllables were Swedish words, in an *AABA* form. Every "A" phrase was lyrically identical. The "B" eight bars translated it for our understanding: a boy and girl sat by a stream and had a dream.

In 1943, "Deep in the Heart of Texas" put the Lone Star State a musical notch higher, with typical Texas pride. It is an AAA tune, and the first four bars of each "A" are almost musically identical to the following four bars of the same phrase. In spite of its repetition, the public found it appealing because of their participation: each "A" phrase includes four handclaps performed twice by the listeners.

Perhaps our biggest novelty hit was in 1943 with the Drake-Hoffman-Livingston tune entitled "Mairzy Doats." It is an *AABA* song. Each "A" phrase lyric was identical; its jumbled nonsensical syllables were explained in understandable words at the bridge. Note that only sixteen bars of lyrics were required because the "A" lyrics were repeated twice. The "B" words were different.

"Mairzy Doats" was a musical household habit; everybody loved it. It is a play-on-pronunciation concept which made its creators all but national heroes.

"Ballin' the Jack" (probably our first novelty tune) by Jim Burris and Chris Smith in 1913, and "The Bunny Hug" also found an infectious and affirmative response. The participation by listeners and dancers was surely responsible, then and now, for the popularity of both songs.

Keep in mind that the novelty tune was important to the musical world through many earlier years. Might it not be time and the musical marketplace right for another novelty hit? Several songwriters reached career highs, because they had these black notes on white paper and cute lyrics in their pockets.

You be the judge. Second only to your creative talent, time is your most important possession. Spend it where you think the opportunities are greatest for fun and success.

Using that "nutty idea" may be the smartest thing you ever did!

D. WORDS . . .

CHAPTER NINE

WRITE THE RIGHT WORD
or Is "Always" an "Eternity"?

Long before there was printed matter, minstrels and poets and storytellers traveled from hamlet to village. They entertained the local populace with legend and words and music.

An engaging mental picture is to see our professional forebears seated before an audience around a fire. To envision their listeners wide-eyed in amazement, smiling in enjoyment, concerned in dramatic worry, and enthralled at the presentation is to understand the success of our counterparts a few centuries ago.

How much easier we have it today! With better facilities, media, and arenas, ours is an infinite opportunity to entertain a national—even international—audience.

But the goal hasn't changed. We still are required to entertain.

As lyricists, we tell a story set to music. That message has dimensions, just as our musical form does. We will see those parameters in later chapters. Now let us improve our ability to tell the best possible story.

Every word creates an image.[1] The difference in words meaning the same thing—or almost the same thing—may be small. But we cannot be vague. In a limited number of words, we must not only be definite but we need to be exactly exact. For instance, are we talking about "sundown" or "twilight"? The mood of our song makes only one of these word-times correct. What is the precise point which we want to—and must—emphasize?

---

1. The immortal Ernest Hemingway said that each word must add something to his story. If it didn't, he deleted that word.

To some degree our melody will help dictate which of two possible words with essentially the same meaning is the better to use. If the tune is upbeat (with perhaps a hundred words in the lyric), that will give us an indication. If only fifty words are present (with lots of long notes on which to hang words), we must be precise; the listener has several musical counts on "hold" notes to hear (and subconsciously consider, like, or dislike our word choice). We must be specific.

When faced with this decision which of the words on each line should you use?

tiny, small, little, minute.
big, large, huge, enormous.
happy, glad, delighted, thrilled.
always, forever, eternity, unending.
sad, blue, morose, disappointed.
mad, irritated, irked, angry.
good, keen, great, excellent.

Some words seem natural in lyrics. Many are not. In studying the above possibilities, we will probably discard "enormous," "excellent," "huge," and "morose." Perhaps in a musical score these words might be appropriate. In a single popular song they won't be our best choices. Why? They are unpoetic, have too many syllables, are hard to rhyme, and just don't fit into common language as well as other words do.

Endearing terms were popular a generation ago. "Dear," "sweetheart," and "darling" have joined high-button shoes and the buggy whip in history. Today they sound cloyingly sentimental with a "sugary" ring to them. They are not in popular usage and tend to conjure in the listener's mind a "filler" word or a struggling effort toward making lyrics rhyme.

Syllable stress is adamant. Suppose you are writing an AABA song. In the first "A" is the word "without." In the following "A", on the same two musical notes, is the word "doubtful." The stress, as established by "without," is on the second syllable. To use these words in parallel musical phrases on the identical notes with identical time values is to throw your song out of emphatic balance.

Some songwriters blithely toss in such stress-contrasting words, and hope for the best. There have been popular songs which got by with this treatment, usually because the recording artist cheats a little on the actual time value, and the difference is not noticed. Don't do it! Be a meticulous lyricist who doesn't cheat.[2]

Here are additional examples of words which will not emphatically scan if you try to match them on parallel "A" phrases:

*Feb*ruary	Sep*tem*ber
*home*coming	ob*jec*tion
*broth*erhood	here*af*ter
a*larm*ing	yester*day*
*nev*ermore	com*plete*ly
*hap*pily	im*pos*sible
Thanksgi*ving*	*Christ*mas

There is no way, without cheating, that a lyricist or a performer can match up these words. Be a better musical poet; don't try cramming them in to fit. They don't and won't. Nine times out of ten you can find the correct matching emphatic word. And if you can't, forget that tenth possibility which sounds forced and unnatural, and start over on another song.

If words must be precise in stress, a phrase may be less so. Note these short three-word phrases. The accent can be on any of their singular syllables. Your melody will perhaps inform you as to their emphasis:

I love you.
Now and then.
You and I.
When you're here.

---

2. I was asked by my talented friend Harold Baker Lyon, to collaborate with him on several songs. We spent hours as he drank soft drinks, smoked cigarettes, and paced the floor pondering which of the grammatical conjunctions "if" or "but" was the better word. His deliberate thoughtfulness over each word and every punctuation mark (he was equally meticulous in his choice of a comma or semicolon) was a lesson to me to rewrite, look it over, check it again, review it—and then do it all one more time!

Lyrics don't just tell your story. They must add an important element of drama to it. That image will create very real interest by your audience in your song.

Suppose you are faced with a choice. We lyricists are, because we can write our song in any direction we choose. Note the differences in these phrases which you might be considering:

Love won't go away / love won't hurry away.
I've only got a minute / I've got a little while.
There are a million reasons/there is just one reason.
Now that I think / I think that now.

Look at the variance in the possible, probable, and positive. Each phrase tells a different story. Be sure it is the story you want to tell by choosing the correct word:

If she loves me.
I think she loves me.
I know that she loves me.

A negative or positive approach can hang on a single word. Note these contrasts:

If she kisses me / if she doesn't kiss me.
What if I do? / What if I don't?
I am going / I won't go.

The dramatic question posed in lyrics is a good audience attention-getter. In an AABA song, your message can be subjectively "how much I love her." In the "B" (bridge) phrase, you might state this possibility: "What if she doesn't love me?" In the final "A", you can resolve it with "Of course she does, and we will live happily ever after." Or you may choose the negative ending: "She doesn't love me, and I am blue."

They tell us that plays aren't written; they are rewritten. So are lyrics. Say what you mean and mean what you say. Your audience will appreciate your efforts because you have chosen the exact words which tell your precise story.

"Always" may not be an "eternity."

CHAPTER TEN

PLOT YOUR LYRICS
or Meet, Like, Love

As children we were read stories which started out "once upon a time" with exciting adventures of a princess and a knight in shining armor. We worried our young minds as the heroine faced such obstacles as a storm, being lost in the woods, a wicked witch, or a fire-breathing dragon. Would the knight save her? Again—finally!—he appeared, rescuing the princess from all dilemma, and they lived happily ever after.

Playwrights know why people go to the theatre: to worry. As a play opens, we are introduced to the characters. The plot develops and the situation worsens: The boy and girl have an argument, the love match becomes a triangle, or the hero can't play in the championship game. These complications become a crisis before they are resolved, then the concern of the theatergoer is rewarded.[1]

Another axiom from the playwright's manual is this: Introduce the characters in the first act, get them up a tree in the second act, and have them slowly struggle to get down successfully by the end of the third act.

When we write a song, the listener gives us about a hundred words with which to tell our story. How can we say our message-set-to-music in that limited time, as compared to two hours of a play's dialogue? Can we present our characters, show their mutual affection, place them in complications, and have them go off hand in hand into the sunset? We can, in a very concise and condensed manner.

---

1. For additional information on plotting, see chapter 27, "Writing a Musical Stage Score."

Not all songs need plotting in this sense. Many of them say "I love you," then state several more reasons why love-does-abound-when-you're-around in a total of thirty-two bars. An excellent example is "Tea for Two." This classic by the great Irving Caesar contains no crisis. Its affirmative story is a continual explanation of why we will be happy together.

The same is true in a negative love lyric which has no plot. It says "you-ain't-here-and-I-wish-you-were-'cause-I-love-you-for-sure." The lyrics tell why she can't love him, listing a series of specifics throughout the song. Superb examples are "Ev'ry Time" (from Martin and Blane's entertaining *Best Foot Forward)* and "Ev'rything Happens to Me."

Even in these two cases where plotting per se is not necessary, the proper telling of a story remains important. Your lyric line must be coherent through a progression of incidences or examples or illustrations. Progress your musical tale with why I love her (a) a little, (b) considerably, (c) completely. Or, conversely, state why things get increasingly worse because she doesn't love me. Remember the old adage: We learn to crawl before we can walk before we can run. To say it another way, introduce your story at the start, tell more about it, and conclude it with definite finality at the end. A carpenter builds a house from basement to roof. So must we "build" a song.

Study your lyrical message. If it is to say "meet, greet, like, love, marry, live happily ever after," it needs to be in that exact order.

In eighty-seven words, a four-legged critter overcame a nasal problem to emerge as a Christmas hero. Who did it? Johnny Marks with his supremely plotted "Rudolph the Red-Nosed Reindeer."

From hello-to-forever is "Polka-Dots and Moonbeams." This is an equally excellent example of lyric plotting.

"What Is There to Say?" has no complications, but plot-builds its lyric message in an outstanding fashion.

One of the all-time simple-but-great love songs is "Surrey with the Fringe on Top" from *Oklahoma!* It is superbly plotted. Its three stanzas, each of which can stand by itself, are a message-in-music triumph.

Ralph Blane's "You Are for Loving" from *Meet Me in St. Louis* is especially noteworthy. It states all of the attributes for devotion, then has a surprise ending: I wish I were good enough to be worthy of your love, but I'm not.

"Chattanooga Choo-Choo" and "Kalamazoo" are also well-plotted songs.

These standards deserve your study. They tell a story, with or without a complication, from an inciting/beginning point through more serious reasons and steps to an ultimate conclusion.

Take a lesson. Copy the examples set by these deans of the songwriting profession who tell us a story with their magnificent lyrics. Do as they have so successfully done: Plot your song.

CHAPTER ELEVEN

LYRIC WORD QUANTITY
or Sing It Simply and Sit Down!

Question: What is the proper number of words in a hit song?

Answer: As few as possible.

To put it another way, state your subject and tell your story without verbosity. Or get the point across briefly and quit!

Whether speaking or writing, Americans have a bad habit: We don't know when to stop. We overstate, repeat, duplicate, become redundant, and otherwise bore our audience by an overkill of words...just as this sentence does. As lyricists, too many of us continue that unforgivable characteristic. We must deliver our message in simple terms and minimal phrases. If we do so, more applause will be ours.

Note the remarkably few words required in these hallowed works:

The Lord's Prayer encompasses 56 words.
The Twenty-third Psalm contains only 118 words.
Lincoln's Gettysburg Address has just 266 words.
The Declaration of Independence established America's
    freedom with only 300 words.

A current Department of Agriculture bulletin regulating the price of cabbage contained 26,911 words!

A newspaper article stated, "If a man were to give me an orange, he would say, 'Have an orange!' But trust that transaction to an attorney, he would say: 'I hereby give, grant, bargain, and sell to you all my right, title and interest in, of, and to said orange, together with all its rind, skin, juice, pulp, pits, and all rights and advantages therein, with full power to bite, cut, and otherwise eat of the same, or give the same away, with or without the rind, skin, juice, pulp, or pits, anything hereinbefore and hereinafter, or in any other deed and/or deeds, instrument and/or instruments of whatever nature and/or kind whatsoever to the contrary in any way notwithstanding.'"

What is that verbiage all about? Nothing, really, more than was originally contained in one sentence: "Have an orange." We have been overdosed in unrequired words.

Heed those examples; delete, omit, and remove the unnecessary. If you don't, you delete your audience because it has become disinterested in etc., etc., and etc.

Communications experts tell us that there is a specific limit to the number of ideas which can be taught—and retained—in a given brief session. The "communicatee" can definitely learn one point. He can also recall a second point. He can probably understand a third point. But no more.

We can translate this into songwriting terms. A music listener will remember the full meaning of the "A" phrase in your song. He will also understand the "B" and probably fully grasp "C".[1]

It is interesting to study other art forms. Consider these and their verbosity:

> *No words:* Sculpture, pantomime, painting, architecture, classical music.
> *About twelve words:* A one-panel cartoon.
> *Some twenty-five words:* A newspaper comic strip.
> *Around 100 - 110 words or less:* Popular songs.
> *Many:* Opera, publications, stage plays, movies, radio, television.

We are not equating the silent art of sculpture with the required talkativeness of television. Yet the illustration is clear: You can't be wordy and be a successful lyricist. In thirty-two-or-so bars, you must tell a complete musical story. Do so—quickly, simply, and briefly.

---

1. It is my opinion that this is a major reason why our popular music has the forms it does: AABA, ABAC, and ABAB. It further explains why a verse containing introductory material is rarely heard today because it is a "fourth point," not repeated for retention and not very important to your story. Since a tag is usually a repeat and does not add new subject matter, we employ it because it helps audience retention.

On every song you write, check—and double-check again—for superfluous words. If my experience is any help, you can eliminate 10 percent of your words and still deliver your lyrics with full meaning.

We hope that this lyric principle—and it *is* a principle—is clear: the correct number of words in a song is the fewest words possible.

Let's be more definite. Exactly how many words is that?

Just as in every song-content area we have studied, this is a variable. In our analysis, we found the high-and-low word limits which provide us a fairly specific boundary. What are those songs and their word quantities?

The number of words consists of between forty in "I'll Be Home for Christmas" and several hundred in "Soliloquy." (The latter is a handsome song, if not a "hit" by public acclaim. Perhaps its wordiness kept it from being such.)

"The Trolley Song" is also at the far end of the wordiness scale. It is a popular classic, even if it tells its well-plotted story at length.

Those songs set the limits. We should follow their creators who have stated their messages in precise terms with minimal words. For examples:

Song	Number of Words
"I'll Be Home for Christmas"	40
"The Sweetest Sounds"	54
"You'd Be So Nice to Come Home To"	55
"White Christmas"	56
"My Ideal"	59
"Embraceable You"	61
"Too Young"	62
"Small Hotel"	63
"I Can't Give You Anything but Love"	64
"Day by Day"	71
"All the Things You Are"	72
"Pennies from Heaven"	74
"Easter Parade"	76

Song	Number of Words
"Candy"	78
"Rudolph the Red-Nosed Reindeer"	87
"Stardust"	97
"Tea for Two"	99
"Over the Rainbow"	104
"The Christmas Song"	107

If current songs tend to be wordier, remember that these acclaimed standards have entertained perhaps three generations of America's musical public. That fact reaffirms this paramount postulate: State it simply by keeping your song short.

CHAPTER TWELVE

RHYMING
or June, Moon, Soon, Tune, Yoon—Yoon?

What do rhymes do for your lyrics? They help the listener remember your song. It is much easier for us to recall a tune whose lyric phrases end in "away," "day," and "stay" than it is to remember consecutive unrhyming lines of "forever," "tomorrow," and "winter." Rhymes also entertain and bring enjoyment to the listener.

Rhyming is easy for a prolific lyricist, but even the most gifted wordsmiths need help. Regardless of how talented you are, you may be stumped occasionally when looking for that exact word. Get some assistance, and use it. Recommended are Roget's *Thesaurus, The Dictionary of American Slang* by Wentworth and Flexner, *Wood's Unabridged Rhyming Dictionary* by Clement Wood, *A Dictionary of Similes* by Wilstach, and other such valuable references. Ask your librarian for additional publications.

This will explain the rhymes in the following illustrations. Each number denotes a two-bar lyric phrase and relates to the last word in it. For example, 1, 2, 1, 2 is the rhyme scheme used in "Stars Fell on Alabama." It shows that the third line rhymes with line 1, and the fourth line rhymes with line 2.

Another example is X, 2, 3a/3b, 2. "What Is There to Say?" utilized this form; X doesn't rhyme with any following line, 2 is the second line ending word, 3a/3b means that there is an internal rhyme scheme (which is a rhyme both halfway through line 3 and at the end of it), and the final 2 shows that line 4 rhymes with the second line.

Look at 1, 1, 1, X in "Without a Song." The second and third lines rhyme with the last word in the first line, and the X does not rhyme.

For a final example: 1, XR, 1, XR in "Pennies from Heaven" indicates that the third line rhymes with the first line, that the second and fourth lines do not rhyme (X), and the "R" means a repeat of the last word in the second and fourth lines. (Your editor is too long removed from his collegiate English courses to recall how grammarians properly defined rhyming phrases and techniques. This system is a workable explanation for our purposes.)

Here are rhyme schemes employed in the opening "A" phrase by songwriters in their hits:

1a/1b, 2, 2, X: "September in the Rain."

XR, 2, XR, 2: "The Best Things in Life Are Free."

X, 2, X, 2: "Night and Day"; "A Foggy Day"; "Moonlight Becomes You"; "Over the Rainbow"; "Rudolph the Red-Nosed Reindeer"; "Have Yourself a Merry Little Christmas."

XR, 2, 3, XR: "Don't Blame Me."

1a/1b, 1, 1, X: "Tea for Two."

1, 1, X, X: "Ghost of a Chance."

1, 1, 1, X: "Without a Song"; "Sweet Lorraine"; "Ev'rything Happens to Me"; "You Are for Loving".

1, 2, 1, 2: "Stars Fell on Alabama"; "I'm Just a Girl Who Can't Say No"; "The Christmas Song."

1, 1, 3, 3: "Dancing on the Ceiling"; "Polka-Dots and Moonbeams"; "This Is the Army, Mister Jones."

X, 2, 2, X: "Fine and Dandy"; "Once in a While"; "Did I Remember?"

1, XR, 1, XR: "I Thought About You"; "Pennies from Heaven"; "I Can't Give You Anything but Love."

XR, 2, XR, 2: "Sentimental Journey"; "Ev'rytime We Say Goodbye"; "Moonglow"; "Gone with the Wind"; "Blue Skies."

X, X, 3a/3b, X: "Stardust."

X, 2, 3a/3b, 2: "What Is There to Say?"

1, 1, 3a/3b, X: "How Long Has This Been Going On?"

XR, XR, XR, X: "Candy."

X, 2a/2b, 3a/3b/2, X: "Thanks for the Memory."

In some songs there may be a final word or syllable on the last count or two of a line. It may be a lead-in pickup word for the following lyric line. Still the rhyme has been clearly made, which is the important point.

You can see that there are few limitations in rhyme patterns. However, the first "A" phrase does not tell the whole rhyming story. Some songs with few or no rhymes in the first eight bars employ rhyming words in following "A" phrases. That offers a definite and enjoyable advantage to both listener and songwriter. Note the following:

> "These Foolish Things" is 1, 1, X, X. It is AABA in form. The third line rhymes in each "A" eight-bar phrase.
>
> "Candy" is XR, XR, XR, X. But the second "A" in this AABA song has three rhyming lines (plus one repeat) and really gets into rhyme, differing considerably from the initial eight-bar absence of it. Line 4 in this "A" also rhymes with X in the initial "A" portion.

If they are so important, are there hit songs which have had few rhymes—or perhaps none at all? That answer is a resounding yes! Look at these examples:

"Moonlight in Vermont" has not one single rhyme in its entire twenty-six bars and four-bar tag total. (Note its unusual form. While it is AABAt, its measure count is 6-6-8-6-4t, for thirty bars.)

"Summertime"; "April in Paris"; and "All the Things You Are" are X, X, X, X. They have their first rhyme in the fifteenth bar, rhyming with the final word in their seventh bar.

"Ol' Man River" is X, X, X, X. No rhyme appears until the twelfth bar, when it rhymes with the line before it in the tenth bar. It occurs in the second "A" for a 1, 1, X, X in that phrase.

"Day by Day" is also X, X, X, X. Its first rhyme is the eleventh and fifteenth bars. Its second eight-bar phrase is X, 2, X, 2 in this ABAC song.

"Don't Blame Me" is 1R, X, X, 1R. The initial rhyme appears in the twelfth bar of this AABA song, and it rhymes with 1R.

"Stella by Starlight" is again X, X, X, X. The first rhyme appears in the "B" phrase of this ABCD song. That section's rhyme pattern is 1, 2, 1, 2 which is quite a departure from the initial eight-bar "A". These rhymes are in the tenth and fourteenth bars and eleventh and fifteenth bars.

"Where or When" completes its initial rhyme in the ninth bar, rhyming with a word in its sixth bar. It has no rhyme in the bridge.

The second "A" in "My Funny Valentine" has its first rhyme in the ninth and eleventh bars, and a thirteenth-bar rhyme with its seventh bar, to form this pattern: 1, 1, X, X. "White Christmas" is identical in rhyme structure.

We can draw several conclusions. These rhyme observations are readily apparent:

1. The vast majority of hit songs use rhymes. They help the listener to learn the lyrics because they are entertaining.

2. Rhyming lyrics early in a song, or later, or in between, or any time adds to audience retention.

3. We have discussed some two dozen different rhyme schemes. It is obvious that all of them work.

4. The most frequently used, and therefore the most popular, rhyme schemes are these:
   X, 2, X, 2: "Night and Day"
   1, 1, 1, X: "Without a Song"
   1, 2, 1, 2: "The Christmas Song"
   1, 1, 3, 3: "Polka-Dots and Moonbeams"
   1, XR, 1, XR: "I Thought About You"
   XR, 2, XR, 2: "Sentimental Journey"
   X, 2, 2, X: "Fine and Dandy"

5. While internal rhymes are clever and sophisticated, they are infrequently employed. Is it because they are more difficult or just not popular? Probably the first answer is correct.

6. Many songs have been standout successes with minimal rhyming, or rhymes coming after their initial "A" phrases.

7. Rhymes tend to come later in other-than-AABA songs.

8. When lyrics rhyme in "A", similar rhyme patterns are expected in the following "A's". Listeners expect them and are disappointed if they are absent. (That is a negative reaction you must avoid.)

9. If your first "A" phrase has few or no rhymes, your song will gain interest if the following "A's" rhyme. Examples shown are "Candy"; "Ol' Man River"; "Day by Day."

10 Rhymes add to listener enjoyment. They are fun to hear and sing.

A not-exact rhyme[1] is no longer a negative quality in a song. A generation ago a rhyme had to be precise; there were few or no liberties taken. Today's hits are less strictly structured. We see frequent examples of "almost rhymes" such as these: "mine/time," "gone/alone," "hand/man," "together/forever," "again/been," and "letter/matter." They aren't perfect rhymes, but the fact that they are close is a help toward retention. And other than entertainment (which is what a song is all about), even this near-miss word rhyming can still be important to us.

The most frequently used rhyming words tend to be one-syllable. The reason is obvious: they are easier to rhyme. We see many more times the rhyming of "he/she" than we do "hesitation/situation."

What are the most popular rhyming words used in lyrics? Here are many which continue to appear throughout the history of popular music:

> day, May, okay, say, stay, way.
> June, moon, soon, tune.
> clear, dear, here, near, year.
> bell, spell, tell, well.
> aglow, go, know, so, sew.
> care, share, there, where.
> by, cry, good-bye, hi, I, my, sigh.
> again,* pain, rain, remain, sane.
> all, call, fall, small, tall.
> blue, do, hue, new, too, view, you.
> dove, glove, love, of.
> furry, hurry, scurry, worry.
> borrow, sorrow, tomorrow.
> again, men, then, when.

---

1. It has been said that there are only three non-rhyming words in the everyday English language—"month," "orange," and "silver." That leaves us an infinite number of words!

be, he, see, she, tree.
around, found, renowned.
down, frown, gown, town.
about, doubt, out, without.
ever, never, weather,* whether.*
embrace, face, grace, place, space.
bright, might, night, right.
await, hate, late.

If you are wondering, spelling has nothing to do with rhyming. "Away" and "obey" are a perfect rhyme. Their last syllable has the same "a" sound. That is the important thing, and not that the sound has a different spelling.

"Pair" and "care" is a perfect rhyme. So is "their/share," "pear/there," "blue/do/you/few/to/through/view," "doubt/without," "where/tear/mare," "tune/moon," "stuff/tough," "year/here," "my/sigh," "worry/hurry," "women/swimmin'," "go/stow/sew," "rain/sane," "believe/receive," "he/tree," "love/of," "way/neigh," "write/bright/height," "wait/straight/-freight/gate," and "gone/on" and on. . .and on. . . .

Businesses as well as songwriters recognize the appeal of rhymes. Note these titles of going commercial activities: Curls 'N' Swirls Hairdressers; Dips 'N' Sips Cafe; Kelly's Deli; Weeds and Beads Clothes; Hats and Spats; and Knit to Fit Knitshoppe.

Study other songs for additional rhyming ideas. See how your songs compare or contrast. This effort will reward you as a more knowledgeable and well-versed—if you will pardon that play on words—lyricist.

---

*Not exact rhyming words but within usable limits.

CHAPTER THIRTEEN

ALLITERATION
or Songwriters Sense Successful Subjects

What is this five-syllable word all about? It sounds like something contagious out of a medical journal or, worse, a government publication. Does it really belong in a songwriting treatise?

You bet! Alliteration is the repetition of the first sound in a series of words. Children learn that "Peter Piper picked a peck of pickled peppers" and "she sells seashells by the seashore." They were easy to learn—if fun and difficult to say—because they are alliterative.

By all means do not use such tongue twisters as those. No one could sing them. (On second thought, they both might make good lyrics for a novelty song.) Nonetheless, they are excellent examples of this grammatical convention.

Lyricists are learned in utilizing the advantages of alliteration in many hit songs. (That is an unwieldy sentence; we used it just to show two instances of alliteration.) As in title repetition, this technique is a vital assist in listener retention. Note these examples: "Baubles, Bangles, and Beads" from *Kismet*; "Rudolph the Red-Nosed Reindeer"; the lyrics of "It's D'Lovely." Another example is the title of this chapter.

A broadcasting executive friend, Ken Heady, is a poet of note. His magnificent magic and wisdom with words (there are two quick alliterative phrases) has brought him high acclaim, both on the printed page (and that's another example of our subject) as well as the speaking platform. With permission, we quote his poem, "December's Dart," so that you can see his appealing use of this grammatical form.

> The wicked whip of the wailing wind
> clashes the snowy land.

The barren boughs of the trembling trees
     sway like a skeleton hand.
The sparrow hungrily searching food
     soars in a frantic flight.
The dim day dies in the clattering cold
     and the wind wails on through the night.

Alliteration does not, for our purposes, require the same sound at the beginning of every consecutive word. There can be other intervening sounds, which this poem clearly illustrates. However, the more frequently we use the same sound, the more we increase the chances of retention by our listeners.

Is it still true alliteration if we employ the words "knife," "gnaw," "know," "knew," "pneumonia," "pneumatic," and "gnat"? We beg the question as to whether it is "true" or not. All of these words have the "n" sound and can be employed alliteratively to serve our needs.

This same logic applies to the use of "phony," "wrong," "psychology," and "ptomaine," which have "f", "r", "s", and "t" sounds.

Eightn't Inglish a phunny ptongue!

Look at the use of alliteration in commercial activities. You may have seen such signs on shops: Treasures and Trivia, Plant Potpourri, Anchor Antiques, Collector's Corner, This 'N' That.

Alliteration is a helpful gimmick. Use it as other songwriters have to make hits of their songs.

One final thought: Would Johnny Marks' great Christmas tune enjoy the same annual popularity if his title was not alliterative? Answer for yourself: sing "Herman the Pink-Nosed Reindeer!"

E. THE ANATOMY OF A SONG

CHAPTER FOURTEEN

SONG FORMS
or Cut Your Pattern to Fit the Cloth

Somewhere, somehow, over a period of years, songwriters learned and developed several predominant song forms which listeners appreciate most. As we determined and understood this public preference, we conformed our efforts to gain that acceptance and appreciation.

If this statement seems constricting to your free-flowing talent and limiting to your creative genius, don't let it. The public makes requirements of producers in every professional field. Look at these product requirements which the buyer "dictates":

1. A clothing manufacturer makes suits for men. Because of buyer demand, he cannot design a coat with three sleeves. His coats have two sleeves, then he adds his own flair to have them stand out among other suits. They adhere to the current fashion.
2. An architect designing a house knows that he has a plot of land only so big. He can't extend beyond its boundaries. If homebuyers want ranch houses, he would err to construct a two-story colonial. He builds a ranch house with a little more zip and appeal than those next door but which conforms to what prospective purchasers are buying.
3. An artist seated before a canvas measuring two feet by three feet can't paint a picture five feet by six feet. Within those dimensions he paints a picture with his personal touch to make it the best painting on the market.

For those same reasons, we confine ourselves to a form desired by popular music buyers. And we follow rules regarding them. These stipulations are dictated by what America sings and musicians play and artists record and charts list.

As songwriters we must answer the wishes of the listening public, or they will applaud music of songwriters who do so instead of ours. That paramount rule applies to both lyric content and musical pattern.

Most songs state their message-set-to-music in thirty-two bars. The majority of them are in four eight-bar phrases. Some have subphrases of four bars, and even sub-subphrases of two bars. In nearly every instance, the total is an even number.

The popular song has specific parts. There may be a *verse*, which is a lead-in. It is not just a musical introduction but part of the whole song. It is related to the *chorus* and sets the stage for it. For more information see chapter 16, "The Verse."

There may also be a *tag*, a little afterthought finale for a strong ending. That subject is discussed in chapter 17, "The Tag Ending."

The major portion of the song is the *chorus*. Here is where it gets down to business, where Cole Porter tells us all about night and day in "Night and Day." The chorus is *the* song, for all practical purposes.

There are three principal song forms: *AABA*, *ABAC*, and *ABAB*.

I. *AABA*

As stated, the chorus usually consists of four eight-bar phrases in a thirty-two-bar song. The first phrase is labeled "A". This is the most important musical and lyrical portion of the song. It may be repeated in an identical "A" phrase following the initial "A". Then it goes into new musical territory in the "B" phrase. That section is entirely different from the "A" and is known as the "bridge" or "release." (Chapter 15, "The Bridge," contains data on that subject in detail.) The melody then returns to the original "A". Now we have a song in *AABA* form. It is the most often used structure and actually has only sixteen bars of original music—"A" and "B", of eight bars each. The "A" phrases are identical or nearly so. The *AABA* form has the advantage of greater melody retention; the listener hears the eight-bar "A" three times.

II. *ABAC*

This form also has four eight-bar phrases. After the opening "A", it goes to the bridge "B", repeats the "A", and has a different ending "C". There are twenty-four bars of original music, plus an eight-bar repeat of "A". The *ABAC* structure is more imaginative, adventurous, and perhaps more interesting than the *AABA* form.

III. *ABAB*

After an opening eight-bar "A" melody, there is a different theme following in the eight-bar "B", a repeat of "A", then a repeat of "B". Sometimes the "A" is called the "verse" and the "B" is labeled the "chorus," but don't worry about this terminology. The "B" is usually the stronger of the two phrases, mentioning the title and being the lyric "clincher." The "A" phrase, like a verse, is a stage-setter for the "B".

Are there any rules directing us toward a specific form? Yes, but "hints" is a better word because nothing is sure-fire definite in this area.

Some guidelines which suggest the *AABA* form are these:

1. When the melody returns to the exact note on which it started in the "A" phrase. Examples: "Over the Rainbow"; "Night and Day"; Don't Blame Me"; "How Long Has This Been Going On?"
2. When the "A" phrase ends on the tonic or first note of its key signature. Examples: "My Blue Heaven"; "What Is There to Say?"; "Blue Skies"; "Body and Soul"; "Moonglow."
3. When the "A" phrase ends on a note requiring its harmony to resolve back into the opening chord of the song. Examples: "Ev'rything Happens to Me"; "These Foolish Things"; "Moonlight Becomes You"; "Polka-Dots and Moonbeams"; "Rudolph the Red-Nosed Reindeer."
4. When the lyric message needs more story buildup, is not yet complete, and would best be said again to the same melody. Examples: "Dancing on the Ceiling"; "September in the Rain"; "Sentimental Journey."

You will see that these characteristics may overlap. If two or more "indicators" are present there is further reason to feel that the *AABA* form is the best to use.

We stated earlier that the second "A" in this *AABA* form is identical to the original "A". That isn't always exactly so, and "exactly" is important here. Sometimes the first "A" phrase does not end on the tonic, requiring chord modulation to get back to the starting note. The last bar or two of the eight-bar phrase may be different in the first and second "A", needing a first and second ending of slightly modified note patterns. This small variance is not so diverse as to keep it from being a true *AABA* song. Songs listed in example 3 fall into this category.

When do we use the *ABAC* form? That answer isn't cut-and-dried clear either. When the *AABA* form doesn't fit, another approach/ form is obviously required. Here are several guidelines:

1. The "A" melody ends up the scale on a relatively high note. Examples: "When Day Is Done"; "Fine and Dandy"; "Tea for Two"; "You Stepped Out of a Dream."
2. While melody is generally the controlling factor, the lyrics also have some bearing. If the story line is not complete in the first "A", but new music would help tell it better, the *ABAC* form should be utilized. Examples: "Day by Day"; "Spring Is Here"; "Ev'ry Time We Say Goodbye"; "Deep Purple"; "Time After Time."
3. The lyric message has been so completely stated in the introductory "A" that the song needs a musical contrast. Examples: "Pennies from Heaven"; "Embraceable You"; "Dolly"; "Gone with the Wind"; "Mame."
4. The melody line calls for something new. A contrasting musical theme is needed because a repetition of the "A" phrase would be redundantly uninteresting. Examples: "My Romance"; "Laura"; "Stardust"; "I Thought About You"; "White Christmas."
5. Somewhat similar to example 1, the tune has built to a musical point up the scale from its beginning, and a return to a lower-note melody would be a letdown to the listener. Examples: "A Foggy Day"; "You Stepped Out of a Dream"; "Gone with the Wind."

What musical signals tell us to utilize the *ABAB* form? This is dictated by the lyric point the songwriter wants to stress. When the lyrics serve as an introduction (almost asking a question which needs an answer or stating "reasons why" for a conclusion that demands a definite positive response), the subject matter gets demonstrative emphasis in a strong chorus ("B") following the "A" verse. The "B" is the primary "story" issue to reemphasize in this form. Examples: "It Takes a Woman" (from *Hello, Dolly!*); "Oh, What a Beautiful Mornin'" (the unique waltz-time opener in

Oklahoma!); "Diamonds Are a Girl's Best Friend" (from *Gentlemen Prefer Blondes*); many religious hymns (such as "Onward, Christian Soldiers"); and to go back into history, most of Stephen Foster's songs ("Camptown Races," for instance).

The *ABAB* form has more latitude in overall length than other forms. It usually has two eight-bar phrases. They are always repeated, for a total of thirty-two bars. They may be repeated again, to make it *ABABAB* in forty-eight bars. We have sung each "A" and "B" with twelve and sixteen bars in songs. It remains a true *ABAB* form when it contains only "A" and "B" phrases, alternately repeated, regardless of its total measure/bar count.

In the *ABAB* form, a songwriter must be musically creative for only sixteen bars unless he uses the longer twelve-or-sixteen-bar convention—which is rare. Even so, he needs to compose only two separate musical phrases.

There is one other form we should know. It is the "blues" framework consisting of a single twelve-bar "A" phrase.[1] Its entire melody line is repeated as many times as the composer/lyricist desires without any other contrasting musical phrase. Many of the old Dixieland tunes employed this form, although it has not been on the popular scene lately. Examples: "C Jam Blues"; "Wang Wang Blues."

Even in these several basic forms, not all of them are absolutely "pure" in every song. Some have slight variations, taking a little latitude while staying within these general frameworks which the musical public understands.

On rare occasion the final "A" has the same opening several bars as do both earlier "A" phrases in an *AABA* song. The melody then changes and is different through the remainder of that section. Is it still an *AABA* form? We say no. If half or more of the final phrase is not identical to the previous "A's", then it becomes a "C" phrase.

"Where or When" exemplifies this structure and is *AABC* in form. Its final phrase has the initial two bars of both "A" phrases. In its third measure it makes a slight departure and from that point is not like any part of the song previously heard. (Its measure

---

1. Musicians like it. They often "jam" in it, using the chord progression without any established melody for their harmonic background on which to improvise.

content is unique but "fits," with 10-10-8-12-bar phrases.)

Is "Have Yourself a Merry Little Christmas" *AABA* or *AABC?* Its last eight-bar phrase is identical to the previous "A's" through five measures, then the final three bars are new music. Our judgment is *AABA* in spite of the last and new part in the final "A".

The same logic applies in other than *AABA* songs. The first three eight-bar phrases in "I'm Always Chasing Rainbows" are different, making it *ABC* in form up to that point. The last section commences with a repeat of the first four bars of the "A" phrase. Its final four bars are new, and it becomes an *ABCD* song.

"Autumn in New York" has "A" and "B" phrases. Its third eight-bar phrase is the same opening four bars as the "A", then departs for the last four bars of that phrase, making it a "C". The last eight bars are unique, and the form is *ABCD*.

We mentioned that one of the advantages of the *AABA* form was melody repetition for retention by the listener. The *ABAC* form shares this benefit to some degree, if lesser, when it repeats the "A" phrase.

Even if the last eight bars of "Autumn in New York" make it a "D" phrase, the first four bars are identical to the opening four bars of the "A". The tune profits from that musical similarity. Perhaps it might be best classified as *ABCA/D*.

"The Sweetest Sounds" from Richard Rodgers' *No Strings* has an equally interesting form. In 2/4 time, it is *ABAC* of eight bars each, plus an eight-bar tag. The "B" has the identical three-and-a-half bars of the opening "A". It departs in the last four-plus bars. The second "A" differs from the opening "A" in the seventh bar, yet still is an "A" phrase. The "C" is just that—a completely different melody. The eight-bar tag is new music, repeating the lyrics of the last four bars of "C" in split time for a pronounced and appealing ending. Perhaps "The Sweetest Sounds" needs a more exact form identification. More accurately it could be called *AA/BACt*.

Are there exceptions to these forms? Definitely so, in some magnificent songs. They are comparatively minimal in number but standouts by terms of success. To open your musical horizon and widen the allowable limits of your creative ability, these songs varied from the norm and found immense public acceptance:

Song	Form	Total Bars	Comments
"All the Things You Are"	ABCD	32	Generally acclaimed as the all-time popular classic is this Jerome Kern-Oscar Hammerstein song.
"I'm Always Chasing Rainbows"	ABCD	32	This perennial was taken from a Chopin theme.
"April in Paris"	ABCD	32	A great Harburg-Duke standard, written in 1932.
"My Funny Valentine"	ABCDt	36	This Rodgers and Hart number from *Babes in Arms* has a four-bar tag.
"Ribbons Down My Back"	ABCAt	40	A Jerry Herman tune from *Hello, Dolly!* has an eight-bar tag.
"Diamonds Are a Girl's Best Friend"	ABCD	16	From *Gentlemen Prefer Blondes*, each sixteen-bar ABCD version is repeated with different lyrics.
"Chattanooga Choo-Choo"	AABA	40	Johnny Mercer used a sixteen-bar "B" phrase here.
"The Girl from Ipanema"	AABA	40	Jobin employed the same Mercer form.
"The Sound of Music"	AABA	40	Rodgers and Hammerstein followed suit; the "B" contains sixteen bars.
"It Takes a Woman"	ABAB	16	The "A" phrase consists of two distinct four-bar phrases; the "B" phrase is eight bars. This variance might be termed ABC of four bars, four bars, and eight bars.
"I Get a Kick Out of You"; "Love for Sale"	AABA	64	Each phrase of these Cole Porter standards is sixteen bars instead of the conventional eight-bar style.
"Cabaret"	AABA	56	This Kander-Ebb song from *Cabaret* employed sixteen bars in each "A", only eight bars in "B".
"Deep in the Heart of Texas"	AB	8	Both the "A" and "B" phrases of four bars each are highly similar, yet there is enough difference to term them "A" and "B". It is repeated twice.

Song	Form	Total Bars	Comments
"Little Girl Blue"	AABA	28	This magnificent Rodgers-and-Hart number from *Jumbo* differs with its final "A" of only four bars.
"Without a Song"	AABA	56	Each "A" of this stellar Vincent Yeomans song has sixteen bars; its bridge contains only eight bars.
"Moonlight in Vermont"	AABAt	26	The bars for each section are 6/6/8/6/4t. This standard has no rhymes in its lyrics (see chapter 12, "Rhyming").
"Moonlight Serenade"	AABA	44	The theme song of the great Glenn Miller Band has a phrase-measure count of 12/12/8/12.
"The Night Is Young"	AABAt	72	In 6/8 time, it is 16/16/16/16/8.
"You Are My Sunshine"	AA	16	This country song was a hit about 1941. It has a second stanza of different lyrics in the first "A" to the same music.
"Pistol Packin' Mama"	AA	16	A big hit in 1943.
"Mack the Knife"	A	16	The 16-bar "A" is repeated thrice in this Blitzstein/Weill favorite. Each repeat is often transposed up a half-step for exciting interest in this 2/4-time tune.
"Summertime"	ABAC	16	This 1935 Oscar Hammerstein minor-key classic from *Porgy and Bess* remains a perennial. Each phrase consists of four bars; the entire sixteen-bar tune is repeated.
"All of a Sudden My Heart Sings"	ABCD	32	Simple, unique, and appealing; its first sixteen bars are the notes ascending the scale, and its final sixteen measures descend in that same order.
"My Ideal"	ABAC	16	A Robin-Whiting standard from the 1930 film, *Playboy of Paris*; each phrase has four bars only.
"I've Got a Crush on You"	ABAC	32	This great Gershwin tune is among the few hits written in 2/4 time.

Song	Form	Total Bars	Comments
"I Don't Know Why"	ABCD	16	A hit of the 1940s.
"Paper Doll"	ABCD	16	The Mills Brothers recording put it on the musical map.
"This Is the Army, Mister Jones"	AABA	56	An Irving Berlin hit in 2/4 meter has phrases of 16/16/8/16 bars.
"Praise the Lord and Pass the Ammunition"	AABA	28	A Frank Loesser 1942 tune, it contains a four-bar bridge.
"Once in Love with Amy"	ABABt	20	Mr. Loesser said it all in four-bar phrases in his soft-shoe-beat song from *Where's Charlie?*
"Where or When"	AABC	44	Rodgers and Hart used 10/10/8/12-bar phrases in this standard from *Babes in Arms* in 1937.
"Happy Birthday"	A	8	This 1893 song by Patty S. and Mildred J. Hill was originally titled "Good Morning to All." It is short, has no rhyme, two title words which are stated four times. How unusual—and popular—can you get?

Worthy of note are these exceptions to the exceptions. Cole Porter's "Begin the Beguine" is long, involved in form, and a classic among classics. "Soliloquy," the Rodgers and Hammerstein standard from *Carousel*, is even longer, more involved, and a truly outstanding song.

Many—perhaps most—of these exceptions are from the musical stage. As you will read in chapter 27, "Writing a Musical Stage Score," the composers/lyricists varied each number in their musical plays. That they did so is praiseworthy; those non-conforming hit songs deserve our consideration and understanding of their form.

What can we learn from our mentors in this area? Some obvious and definite rules regarding song structure:

1. Stay with the standard forms of *AABA*, *ABAC*, and *ABAB*. These patterns are generally what the musical public understands, expects, and enjoys.
2. Depart from these formats if you are writing a musical stage score and need variety in song form.
3. Divorce yourself from these guidelines of eight-bar phrases and thirty-two-bar tunes if the song you "hear" will not conform. But recognize the risk you are taking if you hope for commercial success.

Follow the examples set by the peers of our field. They have proved the methodology toward success. They have also shown when to depart from it.

When all is said, written, and sung, a musical coat has only two sleeves, and the accepted pattern fits the cloth.

CHAPTER FIFTEEN

THE BRIDGE
or Your Song Needs a Musical Vacation

A "bridge" in a song? That is a strange item for a musical composition. Its correct name is "release" but nobody calls it that. Yet it makes sense and is vitally important, funny name or not. We will look at both terms without debating Webster or Funk and Wagnall's technicalities in semantics, and translate it into language we songwriters understand.

As stated in chapter 14, in the *AABA* form we have an eight-bar "A" phrase. Then it is repeated. That repetition gives a listener another opportunity to remember it. He now knows the basic melody (at least we hope so, and experience shows that he does). But to go down that same eight-bar musical road a third time would bore him. How do we keep him interested? We completely change our song at the bridge/release/"B" in every way we can. Our audience needs a musical vacation, and gets it with a different melody and lyric in the bridge.

The bridge must be entirely new. It is required to vary from the original "A" phrase. It is a "bridge"—hence its name—between the second "A" and the final "A". This is true whether your song is in *AABA* or *ABAC* form. To state it in down-to-earth fashion, "go away and come again" is the sole requirement of the bridge.

"Release," in our terminology, means that we let loose of our original melody, the eight-bar "A" phrase. We must depart from it in a definite, dynamic, and dramatic fashion.

How? There are many diverse options we can use.

The best bridge totally divorces itself in every possible musical and lyrical structure from the opening "A" phrase. Whatever we wrote there, we must now write in a completely unrelated manner in the bridge.

Here are some suggestions which will help you to do exactly that:

1. If your "A" phrase has long hold-type sustained notes (half, dotted half, whole), go to shorter time value notes (quarter and eighth notes).

2. If your melodic direction and note flow is generally upward in the "A", reverse it and go down.

3. If you employed adjacent-note melody in the "A", use the interval or any other motion in the bridge.

4. If you were wordy in the "A" with your lyrics, be less so in the bridge.

5. Change the key in which you are writing; transpose it.

6. If your "A" is in major harmony, go into minor at the bridge ("Ol' Man River" is a good example).

7. If your "A" is minor, use the major sound in the "B" (as does "Spring Is Here").

8. If your lyrics rhymed, say, X, 2, X, 2 in your "A", go to a rhyme scheme that is totally different. Or, if you have no rhyme at all (such as in "Moonlight in Vermont"), then rhyme the bridge.

9. Do not (repeat; *not*) mention your title here. "Release" your listener from that, too. (If this suggestion seems contrary to our insisting that title repetition is the best way to have your song remembered—which is true—the listener needs a break from it before hearing your title again in your final "A".)

10. Do everything possible to depart from the first eight bars, which you then repeated, and with which you will end.

The best example of a bridge/release which does everything right to contrast with the preceding "A" portion is "Over the Rainbow". It changes meter, using eighth notes instead of longer-value notes in its "A". It employs repetitive motion, differing from the interval motion in the "A". It is wordy, departing from the few-words style utilized in the "A". This outstanding bridge is in definite and pleasant opposition, both in melody and lyrics, to its "A".

We find the same wide variety of bridge rhyme-schemes that we did in the "A" phrases. These songs are excellent examples which have bridges departing in rhyme form:

Song	"A" Rhyme Scheme[1]	"B" Rhyme Scheme[1]
"I Thought About You"	1, XR, 1, XR	1a/1b, 2, 3a/3b, 2a/2b
"Ghost of a Chance"	1, 1, X, X	1a/1b, 2, 3a/3b, 2a/2b
"Candy"	XR, XR, XR, X	1, 1, 3, 3
"Dancing on the Ceiling"	1, 1, 3, 3	1, 2, 1, 2
"Don't Blame Me"	XR, 2, 3, XR	X, 2, X, 2
"Polka-Dots and Moonbeams"	1, 1, 3, 3	1, 2, 1, 2
"Blue Skies"	XR, 2, XR, 2	1, 1, 2, 2
"Tea for Two"	1a/1b, 1, 1, X	1a/1b, 2a/2b, 3a/3b, X
"You Are for Loving"	1, 1, 1, X	XR, 2, XR, 2
"Easter Parade"	1, 1, X, X,	XR, XR, X, 4a/4b
"Stars Fell on Alabama"	1, 2, 1, 2	1a/1b, 2, 3a/3b, 2a/2b
"Thanks for the Memory"	X, 2a/2b, 3a/3b/2, X	X, 2, 2, 4a/4b

Do we see any common form in bridge rhyme-schemes? Of these twelve examples, several are identical, but most are not. No pattern predominates, and all of these schemes can and do work.

We find a definite departure in all of these illustrations. There is a pronounced contrast between those rhyme patterns used in the "B" from the rhyme form of the "A" section.

The most drastic and dramatic variance in the bridge is made by changing key. The following table illustrates those musical standards which have advantageously utilized this striking difference:

---

1. There is no relationship between 1 in "A" and 1 in "B". Each "1" refers only to the rhyming of that particular eight-bar phrase, either "A" or "B".

BRIDGE TRANSPOSITIONS—GENERAL CONCLUSIONS

Song	Original Key[2]	Changes Key to	New Key Relation	Bridge Lead Note	Relation to Last Lead Note Before Bridge	Sharp/ Flat Change
"Once in a While"; "Moonlight in Vermont"; "Polka-Dots and Moonbeams"	E flat	G	3rd	D	½ step down	5
"Tea for Two"	A flat	C	3rd	C	same note	5
"I Could Have Danced All Night"	C	E	3rd	E	same note	4
"Body and Soul"	D flat	D[3]	2nd flatted	D	½ step up	7
"Smoke Gets in Your Eyes"	F	D flat	5th sharped	F	same note	4
"All the Things You Are"	A flat	G[4]	1st flatted	D	3rd	6
"Long Ago (and Far Away)"	F	A flat	3rd flatted	A flat	½ step up	3
"Thanks for the Memory"	C	E flat	3rd flatted	E flat	½ step up	3
"I Got Rhythm"	B flat	D	3rd	D	3rd	5

2. These are not, in some instances, the true original keys the composers employed. Each key used is for ease of understanding here.
3. Raise ½ step is often performed on final choruses after musical/band interlude to provide variance from the previous phrase for more drama, excitement, and heightening interest.
4. A musical masterpiece, and a "study/exercise" in transposition, as is "How High the Moon."

Four of these eleven songs go to the key of the third note in the original[5] key. Two change to the flatted third of the original key. While those are the most often used transpositions, all of these key changes provide excellent contrast in a bridge.

In making your dramatic departure from the "A" phrase, you may wonder why one other obvious contrast has been omitted. It is purposely absent. *Don't* change tempo! This has occasionally— rarely—been done in tunes on the musical stage. (I have done it, too, going from 4/4 to 3/4 time. The results were quick to show that it was a mistake.) There is not a single hit song which employed this unconventional technique. Apparently it is too radical; the public cannot "shift gears" in rhythm and return to the original tempo again.

Bridge composition is difficult for some, though not for others. In our Conservatory classes are talented songwriters whose "A" phrases were highly appealing but whose bridges were a warmed-over, non-departing eight bars. Comments from the students were correct: Those bridges didn't get away from the original melody and were inferior to the "A". We found other students of which the reverse was true.

Here is further proof that we need a release not only in popular songs but from other items as well. A radio commercial for Campbell's V-8 juice followed this format. It opened with a little musical tune, praising the product in its lyrics. This jingle was repeated immediately. Then, without music, an announcer spoke about V-8 virtues. Following that, the musical jingle was repeated once more. For the reasons that the musical public accepts and approves of the *AABA* form, the Campbell firm realized its advantages: its story could best be told with this same *AABA* design.

A good song requires a good releasing bridge. Take your listener into new music, lyrics, and form which are unrelated to your "A" phrase. Let him enjoy your original "A" again after a proper bridge change. It is *essential*. Be a "releaser" and a bridge-"builder." Get away with an interesting eight-bar phrase (and get away as far as you can), then come back after an entertaining interlude.

The public will appreciate your song more if you construct it as we suggested earlier: Give it a musical vacation.

---

5. "Original key" is more correctly/technically called "concert key."

CHAPTER SIXTEEN

THE VERSE
or Set Your Musical Stage

What is a verse? To the lay listener it is the playing of a song through once with additional renditions to follow—as in first verse, second verse, third verse. This is tantamount to saying that it is the initial "version" of a tune, that the second "version" will have the identical melody but with different words, as will the third "version."

Such is not a songwriter's definition. The verse is a part of the song, just as the chorus and bridge (and perhaps a tag) are. It is the opening portion, a musical introduction with words before the major lyric message in the thirty-two-bar chorus which follows.

Verses are either eight or sixteen in length, and there is no clear-cut preference. They are unrelated in either lyric or melody to the chorus. The lyrics do not (or definitely *should* not) include the song's title. No part of the verse is repeated later in the chorus.

A verse is seldom written, and heard even less frequently, in current popular music. It was more in vogue a generation ago. Then it served an important function; it "warmed up" a listener, paving the way for the chorus (the "real song"). Apparently today's public is not interested in this musical prelude and wants to get to the musical "point."

The verse remains important in show tunes. Why? Because verses set the stage and give a lead into the musical story. For example:

Rodgers and Hammerstein utilized verses effectively in "I'm Just a Girl Who Can't Say No"; "Ev'rything's Up to Date in Kansas City"; and "Surrey with the Fringe on Top" from *Oklahoma!*

Blane and Martin used this introductory musical foreword to their advantage in "Ev'ry Time" from *Best Foot Forward*;

89

"The Boy Next Door"; "The Trolley Song"; and "You Are for Loving" from *Meet Me in St. Louis*.

Apart from show tunes, the best known verses are usually the result of an outstanding recording by a star vocalist. As stated, the verse is the introductory part of a song. However, that order may not be the rendition heard on a record, which can be either of these arrangements:

1. verse/chorus, as is written, or
2. chorus/verse/chorus.[1]

A verse must be highly appealing (such as "A Foggy Day") for a performer to sing it, as Tony Bennett did in his outstanding recording which was a chorus/verse/chorus arrangement. And there must be adequate time on the record in which to perform it.

Verses are rarely used, but they can be important to a songwriter regardless of their order in rendition.

Unquestionably the best-known verse is that of "Ol' Man River." It is so much a part of the song that this musical standard is rarely if ever heard without it. Why do all singers include it? It is because its lyrics truly set the musical stage; it is melodic and appealing; it "fits" and "belongs." Perhaps a better answer is that to omit the verse from "Ol' Man River" is to leave out an exciting part which we want to hear.

"The Trolley Song" verse is equally important and popular for the same reasons.

Everyone knows "Rudolph the Red-Nosed Reindeer," but probably not one person in a hundred knows that it has an eight-bar twenty-six-word verse.

Can you hum any of these verses? Can you sing their lyrics? Or did you even know that these great standards had verses?

"Night and Day"; "A Foggy Day"; "I've Got a Crush on You"; "Stardust"; "September Song"; "White Christmas."

---

1. Marilyn Maye gave this treatment to "The Most," the opening song of her album *Marilyn . . . the Most,* which I wrote and produced.

Proof of the non-recognition of verses was clearly illustrated when we played them in our Conservatory class. One student correctly named four of them, two students knew three, and the remainder recognized two or less. And all of those mentioned are among the more popular.

Probably the best advice is that verses are not necessary in today's musical market. Write a verse if you wish; it is doubtful that it will be heard, even if your chorus is a chart-buster. But if you are writing a musical play, a verse will accomplish several goals: It will entertain your audience and set your musical stage.

CHAPTER SEVENTEEN

THE TAG ENDING
or Sing It Again, Sam

We songwriters know that the best way to have a listener remember our title is to repeat it, repeat it, then repeat it again. As we discussed under "Song Titles" (chapter 5), repetition is the major technique for retention. To help with that retention process, here is the tag.

What is the tag ending? It is a final phrase after the regular thirty-two-bar complete song; it lets us "say it one more time." It usually consists of four bars. It often is a repeat of the melody, although it does not have to be. It is of special value when a song has a "go-out" title, such as in "I Can't Give You Anything but Love." The tag simply repeats that title phrase.

Frequently singers employ this idea and sing their own added tag, even though it was not originally part of the song. It lets them "peak out" their rendition with a big dramatic ending. If this is a popular convention with performers—even in songs without a written tag—it illustrates how important that opportunity can be to a songwriter; the final phrase heard is your song title.

The best examples of a tag ending are Rodgers and Hammerstein's "Might as Well be Spring" and Irving Berlin's glorious musical salute to our country (which is barely tantamount to our national anthem), "God Bless America."[1]

---

1. Mr. Berlin, a World War I army veteran, felt this song to be a patriotic contribution to the military effort. In February 1940 he transferred all rights to the God Bless America Fund. Its trustees have distributed royalties from it to many worthy causes, including the Boy and Girl Scouts. What a magnanimous gift by this wonderful songwriter to these great organizations in his adopted country!

Of interest is this speculative opinion: "God Bless America" was played so often during the 1976 Republican convention in Kansas City that royalties from it may have amounted to as much as $50,000.

Musically, a tag ending is very simple. It can be accomplished several ways:

1. End the song in a traditional manner as written, then repeat the final four bars. "Might as Well Be Spring" does this, and it doubles the original time values on notes for additional emphasis.

2. "Chattanooga Choo-Choo" is an exact repeat of its final four bars.

3. Instead of the melody ending on the expected tonic, it ends on the fifth (or G in the key of C). Following is a seventh chord to lead into the repeat of the final phrase. "God Bless America" uses this form for two bars, then doubles the time on the final two bars (making it four bars) so that the tag consists of six bars.

4. Rather than end on the tonic, the melody goes up to the sixth note, with the major or 7th chord of that sixth note (VI, or either A major or A7 in the key of C). This is an attention-getting climax "cousin" chord. The tag melody, whose lyrics contain your title, is then usually different from anything previously heard in the song. When artists perform an unwritten tag, this is the method most often used by them.

5. Similar to 4 above, the melody rises to the seventh note, but with the major or 7th/9th chord of the sixth note (VI, with either A major or A7(9) in the key of C). It serves the same exciting purpose in the song. The voice note makes the A major/A7 a ninth, and it is pleasant harmony.

6. This approach is the same as in 4 above, except that the note and chord are the third note/chord in the key signature (III, or E major or E7th in the key of C).

7. "My Funny Valentine" ends on the tonic, but up an octave higher. Its melody has progressed in that direction, suggesting a more-to-come sound; it can't end there. Nor will its chord structure (VI minor, or A minor in the key of C) let it. So Mr. Rodgers resolved his harmony and added a four-bar new-music tag in this great standard.

8. "Moonlight in Vermont" has a four-bar tag with a new melody.

See what a tag does for your song:

a. It lets you repeat your title.
b. It lengthens your tune by four or six or eight bars, still within acceptable limits in addition to a conventional thirty-two-or-so bar chorus.
c. It gives you a bigger, more definite, and dramatic ending.
d. The words of your title are the last words heard by the listener.

These are important benefits for little creative effort. And often the effort is only to repeat what you have already written.

Use the tag ending. Give your song the "one more time" advantage: Have Sam—or Shirley—sing it again.

F....AND MUSIC

CHAPTER EIGHTEEN

MELODY COMPOSITION
or What Is the Best Note to Follow Middle C?

We have a total of twelve tones, each a half-step distance from the other. Those are our musical "bricks" from which to "build" a tune—no more, no less. Out of those dozen sounds have come countless melodies since Adam taught Eve to whistle. With different time values and sequences, the possibilities of your employing these same notes in any original melody remain infinite. To say it another way, the chances of your duplicating another tune (unless you are subconsciously thinking about one) are minute. Therefore, the keyboard scale is your unexplored musical world!

As a songwriter you write a melody, not caring on which note it starts. Whatever is your first note of the song you "hear," that is the right note. We analyzed hit songs to determine where composers commenced their outstanding melodies. The musical starting point was any note in the major scale.

For ease of understanding, we put these examples in the key of C. We disregarded pickup notes, and refer only to the first note in the initial full bar of each song's chorus. Look at these starting notes of songs taken from 144 tunes analyzed:

Note	Songs
C	"Over the Rainbow"; "Dream"; "Too Young"; "Oklahoma"; "The Christmas Song."
D	"Stardust"; "Body and Soul"; "I Surrender, Dear"; "Small Hotel"; "How High the Moon."
E	"White Christmas"; "Chattanooga Choo-Choo"; "Sentimental Journey"; "Easter Parade"; "The Trolley Song."
F	"April in Paris."

95

Note	Song
G	"Rudolph the Red-Nosed Reindeer"; "Hello, Dolly!"; "Night and Day"; "I Got Rhythm"; "Ol' Man River".
A	"Moonlight in Vermont"; "My Ideal"; "My Funny Valentine"; "Embraceable You"; "Blue Skies."
B	"Laura"; Stella by Starlight"; "Dancing in the Dark"; "I've Got a Crush on You"; "I Can't Get Started with You."

Just for the record, it is interesting to study these statistics:

Lead Note	Number of Songs	Percent of Total Songs
C	38	26
D	7	5
E	42	29
F	1	0
G	33	23
A	14	10
B	10	7
Total:	145	100

You will notice that songs with lead notes of C, E, and G (which make up the C major chord) comprise 78 percent of all songs considered. The remaining 22 percent of the songs have lead notes which are found in other C chords.

This does not imply that all songs start on the I major chord (C major chord in the key of C). The vast majority do, but surely not all. (See chapter 21, "Chord Progression.")

Any lead note will serve our purpose, as it has for writers of hit songs.

Where do we go from here in our composition?

We could study each of these 144 songs and provide that answer. Some of them went one note higher, another group went one note lower, others went two notes. We could make the same minute study regarding the third note of a song. We won't, because you can see the myriad possibilities available to you if you stay within the public's singing range.

Now pay particular attention to the following paragraph which is the most fundamental rule of all.

What is the sole proof of a good melody? Your ear. Is the tune pretty? Is it singable? Does it fit your lyrics? If your answers are all *yes* to that brief but critical examination, then you have a good tune. If not—and be honest or you are just kidding yourself because a publisher won't expend funds to lose money if he doesn't find your song marketable—then go back to your musical drawing board. Come up with a tune that will measure up to the "ear test."

There are several musical-scale directions a melody can go. Usually more than one direction will—and should—appear in the same song. Those primary movements/motions are these:

1. *Adjacent-note motion.* Call it "next-door-neighbor-note motion" or "consecutive-note motion" if you wish, because it is also those. It does not jump; the melody line flows easily to the note next to it.

   Examples: "Small Hotel" and "I Get a Kick out of You" both have a first jump between notes in the fifth bar of the song. "When I Grow Too Old to Dream" does not jump until the third bar, jumps in the fourth bar, then stays with its *adjacent-note motion* until the eighth bar; essentially, it has few jumps in its entire melodic line. "Dream" has eighteen consecutive adjacent notes before jumping in its eleventh bar. "White Christmas" departs from its adjacent-note motion note before its eighth bar. (This song is somewhat unique in its *adjacent-note motion*; it also has some *chromatic-note motion.*)

   The best example is "All of a Sudden My Heart Sings." It goes progressively up on the eight notes of the scale, then follows the scale precisely on its downward route.

2. *Interval motion.* Another name for this melodic movement is "jump motion" because it jumps over adjacent notes. Notes do not follow each other in either chromatic sequence (up/down a half step and continuing in the same up/down direction) or harmonic full-step sequence.

   You will have a better understanding of *interval motion* by studying these examples: "Stardust"; "I'm Looking Over a Four-Leaf Clover"; "Have Yourself a Merry Little Christmas"; "Deep in the Heart of Texas"; "Mairzy Doats"; "The Hut Sut Song"; "Slow Boat to China"; "Take Me Out to the Ball Game."

3. *Redundant-note motion.* Term it "ditto" if you prefer. This is a melody with a note struck again and again without other intervening notes. Obviously, it will need some relief; it must have another type of motion. To stay forever on the same note will bore a listener, give him the opinion that you don't know any other notes, and sound like a piano tuner who can't quite get it in tune.

    The best example is "Poor Johnny One-Note." Another is "Surrey with the Fringe on Top," in which its first six notes are the same. So are the opening eight notes in "All of a Sudden My Heart Sings," which continues the same *redundant-note motion* in the next eight notes—but with some relief because the second series of notes are a full step higher. The first ten notes are identical in "Ghost of a Chance"; it does not change notes until its third measure.

4. *Repetitive motion.* This is somewhat related to *redundant motion.* It can be highly effective but needs another motion type to keep from becoming boring. Its best example is the bridge of "Over the Rainbow." That melody line uses alternating repeats of the fifth and third notes of the chord (G and E in the key of C) in its first nine notes before going to eleven adjacent notes which are also repeated alternately; this is also *repetitive motion* as well as *interval motion.*

5. *Chromatic-note motion.* This is an extremely rare musical bird. In "Lover"—the best example—the melodic flow is a half step interval through its first five bars.

These examples prove that all five motion types will and do work. A tune consisting of only one of them will bore your listener. (Exceptions are few; maybe "Stardust" is the best of those, employing *interval motion* throughout most of that classic.) Therefore, if your primary "A"-phrase motion is *interval/jump motion,* utilize a different direction in your bridge. Remember that two motion types can also be appealing in the "A" phrase.

Restrictions are few, and all motions and directions are available to you. Use any of them, as other successful songwriters have.

Perhaps the cardinal rule is one we have already discussed: Release your listener from the sameness in motion of your song at the bridge—which means "bridging" your identical eight-bar "A" phrase with a new and different melodic motion.

Twelve tones, five motion types, three popular distinct forms, and a wide variety of time values provide you with an infinite number of musical ingredients with which to construct a song.

Isn't our musical "equipment" a lot less restrictive than you thought?

CHAPTER NINETEEN

MAJOR? MINOR?
or Often the Twain Do Meet

There are two principal harmonic sounds available in the composition of a song: major and minor. By far the vast majority of standards are written in major keys. A minor-key song is a rarity. That sound is mostly—but not always—utilized when writing to lyrics with a "blue" mood and a negative story.

Virtually every major-key song uses some minor chords for contrast. The employment of all major chords throughout an entire song is unique. There are a limited number of "pure" major-chord tunes. "You Are My Sunshine"; "Rudolph the Red-Nosed Reindeer"; and "Pagan Love Song" are examples.

Songs with all, or nearly all, minor-key chords are equally few. Their examples are interesting:

"Goodbye." This was the slow-tempo moody theme song of Artie Shaw's great band in the 1940s.

"Gloomy Sunday." The lyric is about a lost romance and a resultant death. According to reports, its playing was so depressing that it caused a suicide.

"Summertime." This Kern-Hammerstein classic from *Porgy and Bess* has very few major chords.

"The Thrill Is Gone." George White's *Scandals* of 1931 contained this fine mostly minor tune by Brown and Henderson.

Some songs which are largely minor in chord, composition, and lyric character change to major-key harmony at their endings. Examples: "Yesterdays"; "St. Louis Blues"; "Get Out of Town."

Several minor-key songs go to the major sound at the bridge for appealing contrast. Examples: "Spring Is Here" and "Ribbons Down My Back." (The latter, from *Hello, Dolly!* by Jerry Herman, has yet to receive deserving acclaim. Is it because there are so many fine tunes from that score which eclipse it?)

Conversely, "Ol' Man River" is unique. This philosophical song is in major, goes into minor at the bridge, and resolves back into major for the final "A" phrase.

Not all minor-key tunes have pessimistic lyrics. Cole Porter's "You'd Be So Nice to Come Home To" starts out and mostly stays in minor, employs major-key contrasting chords, goes out major, yet all the while telling us a happy narrative. "Nature Boy" has a minor chord structure and a negative-sounding melody even though its lyric message is on a positive plane. "Summertime" states reasons to be happy and no need to cry in slow "blues" rhythm and minor sound. "The Sweetest Sounds" is equally optimistic, minor harmony notwithstanding. Are they a contradiction between words and harmonic mood? So it seems, yet they "fit" for the listener's pleasure.

Minor chords can be used as substitutes, as brief passing chords, or to present a contrasting effect. They can be well employed in opposition to a predominance of major chords for an enjoyable melody. Utilize them to strengthen a mood, provide harmonic color, and aid your lyrical message.

Use both major and minor chords. More often than not, the twain do meet.

CHAPTER TWENTY

CHORD FORMATION
or R Sharp + W Flat + V Natural = ?

I. BASIC CHORDS

You know how to make chords. This chapter will be a review for you. It is about the equivalent of a six-hour college course in harmony.

Let's look at the C scale. "Scale" comes from the Italian word "scala," meaning "ladder." And we have a "ladder" of notes with which to work. From middle C to an octave above ("octave" is taken from the Latin, meaning eight) is obviously eight white notes. We put numbers on them, and mark them on the treble cleff staff as:

```
C D E F G A B C
1 2 3 4 5 6 7 8
```

Run that over on your piano. It is the C scale, pure and simple.

Now let's take various notes—by numbers—and make chords of them. Middle C is our starting point, and we are in the key of C. You can add the octave/8 in any of these chords, with only a few stated exceptions.

MAJOR. This is *the* principal chord. It is made up of 1, 3, 5, containing the notes C, E, G. The chord symbol is written on a lead sheet as "C" over the melody line this way:

MINOR. It is 1, 3 flat, 5; or C, E flat, G. Write its symbol as "C — " or "Cmin." This chord comes out musically:

SIXTH. This is the major chord plus the sixth note: 1, 3, 5, 6; or C, E, G, A. It is not just an ending/final chord, but does put a sort of musical "period" punctuation mark to a melody. (To help you remember, it contains the same notes by which a ukelele is tuned, although they are in inverted order: G, C, E, A, and the old saw that is sung with them, "My Dog Has Fleas.") On the lead sheet it is "C6"; on the musical staff it is shown like this:

C6

MAJOR SEVENTH. This is a more modern sound than the chords previously mentioned and has been popular for the past thirty-or-so years. (Current harmonies have progressed toward distant sounds; this chord is hardly "far out" by present-day standards.) It consists of 1, 3, 5, 7. Do not repeat the octave (C/8); that note is too close to the 7th (B) for your ear to enjoy. The notes are C, E, G, B. Musicians call it the "Laura" sound, because it is the first chord of that great song, coming on the title word "Laura" after the pickup notes. It is written as "Cmaj7," and scored as:

C maj7

SEVENTH. Its pedigreed name is *dominant seventh*, and it is dominant. Don't (repeat, *don't*) confuse this with the *major seventh* chord just discussed. It is as different from the *major seventh* as day is from night. (We musicians/songwriters should think up a new name so that we don't mistake a *major seventh* for *seventh*.) It is called a "church chord" because it is often found in hymns; of the two-chord "amen" sequence, it is the "a" before the "men." You can't end a melody on this chord (yes, it has been used for effect, but you shouldn't). The ear demands that it has a follow-up resolve into another chord. The structure of the *seventh* is for paving the way into its next chord. It consists of 1, 3, 5, 7 flat; or C, E, G, B flat. Its chord symbol is "C7" and is written:

C7

DIMINISHED. This chord has an unmistakable sound. That is true of every chord, but it is especially so here. It was used in silent-movie days for excitement in a pursuit-chase scene. Pianists played it upbeat in consecutive inversions, running up and down the scale. In upbeat songs today, it has an enthusiastic ring. In ballads, it allows a change of mood, usually to sad or "blue." It is made with 1, 3 flat, 5 flat, 6; or C, E flat, G flat, A. The symbol is "C°" or "Cdim." It is scaled:

There is a diminished chord for every key, of course. However, there are only three separate diminished sounds in this unusual harmonic. The C diminished chord contains the same notes as the E flat, G flat, A diminished chords; F diminished contains the same notes as A flat, B, D diminished chords; G diminished contains the same notes as the B flat, D flat, and E diminished chords. Play them and prove it to yourself.

AUGMENTED. This chord serves the same purpose as the seventh chord—a positive lead-in for the forthcoming chord. It is stronger than a major chord. You can't end on it; your ear won't let you, demanding that it be resolved. (While we have heard song arrangements ending on the seventh which would make a dog howl, there are none ending on an augmented chord.)

It is more modern-sounding than the seventh chord. Claude Debussy, the French classical composer, belonged to the "Impressionist" school and was a protagonist of this progressive chord.

The augmented chord consists of 1, 3, 5 sharp; or C, E, G sharp. An excellent example is in Hoagy Carmichael's magnificent standard, "Stardust." He employs it on the opening pickup notes, where the lyrics read: "Sometimes I . . ." The "I" word-note has the augmented chord, demanding a follow-up resolve into the next chord. Write it as "C+ or "Caug," and score it:

Each key has an augmented chord. But as was explained under diminished chords, there are only three different augmented sounds on the keyboard. The C augmented chord contains the same notes as the E and A flat augmented chords; the F augmented has the identical notes as the A and D flat augmented chords; and the G augmented chord is exactly the same as the B and E flat augmented chords.

NINTH. This is also a modern sound. It is the major chord plus the ninth note. It consists of 1, 3, 5, 9; or C, E, G, D an octave above middle C. Do *not* use the octave (C/8) or you will get a "muddy" sound. On the lead sheet it is illustrated as "C9". Score it this way:

Playing it, you will find that C9 sounds a little vacant, as if something were missing. You can fill it in with an additional note, adding any of these options:

A *sixth.* It will then be 1, 3, 5, 6, 9; or C, E, G, A, D. The chord symbol will be "C9(6)" and is scored:

A *seventh.* It will have 1, 3, 5, 7 flat, 9; or C, E, G, B flat, D. The chord symbol is "C9(7)," and is scored:

A *major seventh.* It will consist of 1, 3, 5, 7, 9; or C, E, G, B, D. The chord symbol is "Cmaj9," and is scored:

These are the fundamental chords which we songwriters use. There are more, just for your information:

1. A minor chord with a (C—6). It is used in that great standard, "September Song."

105

2. A flatted fifth (C♭5). This dissonant chord was big in the early 1950s bebop era when Dizzy Gillespie and Charlie Parker played their innovative sounds.
3. A minor with a major seventh (C—maj7).
4. An eleventh and thirteenth (C11, C13).

Except for the first example (Cmin6), these are "far-out" sounds. You will have rare opportunity to use them. For all practical purposes, *major, minor, sixth, seventh, major seventh, diminished, augmented*, and *ninth* chords will answer every need in your songwriting career.

II. SUBSTITUTION CHORDS

Here is a harmonic concept which will add entertaining variety to your fundamental chords. You are familiar with their construction. There is much to be gained in your songs if you use them. They can be the spice to give your music color and flavor and "zap."

Before we get into the subject further, we should know this basic reference. Just as the notes of the scale have numbers of 1 through 8, the chords of these same eight notes (really seven, plus the octave/8) use Roman numerals to identify them. Here they are:

C	D	E	F	G	A	B	C
I	II	III	IV	V	VI	VII	VIII

A substitution chord is a replacement chord, just as its definition denotes. It takes the place of a principal chord. It sounds similar, yet it is a little different. . .made by either adding or omitting a note. For instance:

1. The *minor* chord of the sixth note in the scale substitutes for the original *sixth* chord. To write it in technical terms, *I major* has as its substitute *VI minor*, or, *Amin* is the substitute for *C6*. To explain it further, *C6* consists of C, E, G, A. *Amin* is made up of the notes A, C, E. The difference is that it leaves out G, or the fifth note of the original major chord.

   Play the primary chord, and follow with its substitution chord (C6, Amin). Hear how they generally sound alike, and note their slight but important difference. Then play them in keys other than C.

Basic Chord	Composed of	Notes	5th Note Omitted	Substitution Chord	Notes
C6	1, 3, 5, 6	C, E, G, A	G	Amin	A, C, E
F6	1, 3, 5, 6	F, A, C, D	C	Dmin	D, F, A
G6	1, 3, 5, 6	G, B, D, E	D	Emin	E, G, B
Bflat6	1, 3, 5, 6	Bflat, D, F, G	F	Gmin	G, Bflat, D

2. The *minor* chord of the third note in the scale substitutes for the original *major seventh* chord. Technically, *I major seventh* has its replacement *III minor*. To state it another way, *Cmaj7* consists of C, E, G, B. The *Emin* chord is made up of E, G, B, which omits C, the first note (tonic) of the original major chord. Play both chords and listen to their slight variance. That is the "zap" we mentioned which substitution chords provide. Look at these examples:

Basic Chord	Composed of	Notes	Tonic Omitted	Substitution Chord	Notes
Cmaj7	1, 3, 5, 7	C, E, G, B	C	Emin	E, G, B
Fmaj7	1, 3, 5, 7	F, A, C, E	F	Amin	A, C, E
Gmaj7	1, 3, 5, 7	G, B, D, Fsharp	G	Bmin	B, D, Fsharp
Bflatmaj7	1, 3, 5, 7	Bflat, D, F, A	Bflat	Dmin	D, F, A

There are many other substitution chords. These listed here suffice for our purposes and give us the sounds we need.

The basic chords will make up the harmonic "skeleton" of any song. Substitution chords can be gainfully employed to add variety for you. Use them and enjoy the "spice" they will bring to your music.

CHAPTER TWENTY-ONE

CHORD PROGRESSION
or Where Do I Go from T Flat Minor?

This title may sound like it came from a book on Advanced Musical Theory. It didn't, and don't let it frighten you. Simply translated, it means moving from one chord to the next throughout a song.

While this data isn't critical, it is a continuation of the "course" in harmony we promised. We have used the word "tonic" in referring to the first note of the scale. All notes have names. To know these names is to understand their harmonic relationship to each other, the strength their presence adds to a chord, and the effectiveness they provide in the structure of a song. Here is the C scale and the names of its notes:

Tone Number	Note	Name
1	C	tonic
2	D	supertonic
3	E	mediant
4	F	subdominant
5	G	dominant
6	A	submediant
7	B	leading tone[1]
8	C	octave

And now you know!

Suppose that we have this chord progression in a four-bar phrase...

First measure: C for four beats
Second measure: F for two beats, D minor for two beats

---

1. Don't confuse this term with "lead note." The latter means the first note of a song or phrase, which is quite different. "Leading tone" means that it leads into the tonic, paving the way for the first note of the scale.

Third measure: G for two beats, G7 for two beats
Fourth measure: C for four beats

On a lead sheet, we would score it thusly:

Each little slant-line mark under the chord indicates one count. Check it against the written explanation and you will see that they match identically.

We can score this same information another way, with the Roman numeral reference to chords as explained. We don't write our lead sheets like this; performers want chord symbols instead. But it does illustrate the reference of chords to each other and their latter/note symbols:

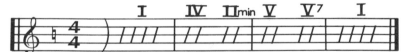

C is I here because we are writing in that key. If we are writing in F (or any other key) the tonic note/chord is always I, and the remaining seven notes are II through VIII/octave.

That is all the background we need. We are ready to absorb this subject in full.

If you are asking yourself "What chord do I use next?" there are several logical possibilities. Let us assume that you are writing in the key of C. Here are some solutions, and one or more will answer this question for you:

1. In all probability, you have opened your song with C major (I), because most songs do so.

---

2. This "natural" sign is not necessary. It is often used by musicians, songwriters, and arrangers to emphasize that there are no sharps or flats in the key signature. Its presence reemphasizes that it is written in the key of C.

2. The best bet is that your next chord will be "in the family." The "family" category is I, IV, V, or C, F, G chords. Since you opened with I (C), your first consideration for the chord to follow is IV (F) or V (G).

3. What is the next note in your melody? Most of the time, the forthcoming chord will include the upcoming note as a part of it.

4. If the next note in your tune is of short time value rather than a longer "hold" note, then the suggestion stated in 3 may be invalid. For example, if your next note is D and is a quick "passing" note with minimal time value, it is doubtful that D will be your next chord.

5. If your melody takes a dramatic change, or comes to a climax, or needs a special sound, try a "cousin" chord: VI, III, VII, II (or A, E, B, D), and in that order.

6. If your melody calls for the next chord to be "in the family" (going from I to IV, or C to F) and you want to have a strong sound leading into it, use a seventh (C7 to F).

7. Under the same circumstances as stated in 6 except that you want a more modern sound, employ an augmented chord (C+ to F).

8. The final chord in your song will be I (C). (I can think of only one song exception to this last-chord rule.)

9. Minor, diminished, sixth, major seventh, and other chords will add variety and color for your song.

If you are still stumped in your search for that next chord and those to follow it, the solutions are many. Look at these chord progressions used by songwriters in the first eight-bar "A" of their hit songs.[3] Again, for the sake of simplicity, we have not always used their original keys, but illustrate all songs in C. They are in 4/4 time, with pickup notes omitted.

---

3. The chord progressions listed may differ slightly from those actually employed by their composers. The lead sheets/sheet music was not analyzed. Some substitution chords may have been used by your author. Basically the harmony is correct and reliable.

"Don't Blame Me": C Bb/A /F G /Cmaj7 / F G /C Bb A /F G+ /C
|| ||/ |||| / || || / |||| / || ||/ || | | / || ||/ ||||

"Stardust": F /F /C+ /F- /C /E- /F /F
||||/ ||||/ ||||/ ||||/ ||||/ ||||/ |||| / ||||

"Over the Rainbow": C A- /Cmaj7 C7 / F Co/ C C7 /F F- /C A A+ /F G G7 /C
|| ||/ ||| | / || ||/ || || / || ||/ ||| | / || | | / ||||

"Moonlight in Vermont": C /Fmaj7 G7 /C /F- / Fmaj7 G7 / C
||||/ || ||/ ||||/ ||||/ ||| | / ||||

"Sunny Side of
the Street": C /E7 /F /G /A- /A7 /F G7 /C
||||/ ||||/ ||||/ ||||/ ||||/ ||||/ || ||/ ||||

"Moonlight Serenade": C /Co /F /F# G G+/C /C /C /A
||||/ ||||/ ||||/ | || | / ||||/ ||||/ ||||/ ||||

"Tea for Two": F G /F G /Cmaj7 C6 /Cmaj7 Co /F G /F G /C /C
|| ||/ || ||/ || ||/ || ||/ || ||/ || ||/ ||||/ ||||

"Body and Soul": D- /F G G7 /C G+ /C Co / F /G Fo/A- G G+ / C
||||/ || | | / || ||/ || ||/ ||||/ || ||/ || | | / ||||

"White Christmas": C /F C B C/F /F# G G7 / F /G G7 /C /C
|||/ | | | |/ |||/ | || | / ||||/ || ||/ ||||/||||

"Have Yourself a
Merry Little
Christmas": C /D-7 G7 /C /D-7 G7 /C A-7 / D-7 G7/ E7 A7 /D9 G7
||||/ ||| | / ||||/ || || / || || / || ||/ || ||/ || ||

"You Are My
Sunshine": C /C G+ G /C /C C7 /F /F G G7/C /C C7
||||/ || | | / ||||/ ||| | / ||||/ || | | / ||||/ ||| |

"Once in a While": C /C /A7 /A7 /F /G7 /C /G G7
||||/ ||||/ ||||/ ||||/ ||||/ ||||/ ||||/ || ||

"Pennies from
Heaven": C /C Co /F G /F G7 /C /C Co /F G /F G7
||||/ || ||/ || ||/ || ||/ ||||/ || ||/ || ||/ || ||

"The Nearness
of You": C /C7 /F /Co /C Bb / A F G7 / C /G G7
||||/ ||||/ ||||/ ||||/ || ||/ || | | / ||||/ || ||

"S'Wonderful": C /C /Go /Go /Fmaj7 /Fmaj7 G7 /C /C G7
||||/ ||||/ ||||/ ||||/ ||||/ || || / ||||/ || ||

"Rudolph the
Red-Nosed
Reindeer": C /C /C /G /G /G /G G7 /C
||||/ ||||/ ||||/ ||||/ ||||/ ||||/ || ||/ ||||

All but three of these sixteen songs use C major (I) as the opening chord. Of the exceptions, two employ F (IV)—note that it is a family" chord—and the other uses D minor (II—, which is a substitution chord for IV/F).

You will further notice that no two chord schemes are alike. There is a wide variance in chord progressions used by hit songwriters. Obviously all of them work.

Observe the predominance of "family" chords in the opening eight-bar phrases of these sixteen songs. The chords of C (I), F (IV), and G (V) appear repeatedly in all of them.

The majority of *AABA* songs have the seventh chord as their last sound in the eighth measure. It gives a strong lead back into the forthcoming and repeating melody—the second "A"—which commences on the tonic/I/C chord in most of them. This is not always true, and definitely won't be the case when the final chord in the first "A" is the same as the opening chord of the second "A" (as happens in "Rudolph the Red-Nosed Reindeer," for example).

There is more to the chord story. The bridge of each song should hold an entirely different pattern of chords, chord quantity, and their few or many changes. Nonetheless, the "A" phrases of these historically popular songs offer you many possible models: And there are lots more that we haven't listed.

In discussing the mechanics of songwriting, a Conservatory student said that she wrote chords first, then developed a melody from them. This method seemed unique to us until we analyzed some hit songs. Whether he did so or not, purposely or accidentally, Hoagy Carmichael's immortal "Stardust" could have been composed in that fashion.

You won't be at a loss with the infinite variety of harmonic patterns available to you. Experiment with them. Write your melody line. Let your ear tell you the best-sounding chords to accompany it. After all, that is the ultimate test in songwriting, isn't it?

CHAPTER TWENTY-TWO

CHORD QUANTITY
or L Sharp Sixth Needs a Break

Get your listening ear ready while we consider this chapter together.

We have discussed the eight basic chords found in every key.[1] We mentioned several advanced chords—a minor sixth, for example—and ninths with added notes. That gives us a gang of chords in our original key, and we have just started.

Suppose we are composing in the key of C. In addition to all of the C chords, we will naturally use the "in the family" chords of F (IV) and G (V).[2] So far, we have over thirty available chords. And that doesn't include substitution and "cousin" chords.

If we want a real contrast in the bridge, we can change key. That gives us new "family" and "cousin" and substitution chords. How many chords is that altogether? More than you thought, a lot, plenty, and more than enough—all of those quick answers.

We won't use that many, and there are good reasons why we don't:

1. The melody line does not require that many harmonic changes, and
2. Too many unnecessary chords can be a detriment to a song, just as too few chords will not give it full color.

We see that at least thirty chords might come easy in a single song, and the possibility of exceeding that number gives us another handful.

In every song content category, we have learned from hit songwriters and followed their format examples. Let's do so again, by studying the chord quantity used by them in the following twenty songs:

---

1. Refer to chapter 20, "Chord Formation."
2. Discussed in chapter 21, "Chord Progression."

Title	Number of Bars	Form	Chords in Each Phrase					Total Number of Different Chords
			1st	2nd	3rd	4th	Tag	
"Poinciana"	32	AABA	5	4	6	5	none	8
"This Is the Army, Mister Jones"	56	AABA	8	8	6	7	none	9
"Amapola"	32	ABAC	4	3	6	7	none	10
"Let's Do It (Let's Fall in Love)"	32	AABA	7	5	10	10	none	13
"Too Young"	32	ABAC	7	7	8	11	none	13
"Manhattan"	32	ABAC	7	9	6	6	none	14
"The Last Time I Saw Paris"	34	ABAC	4	6	9	5	none	14
"I'm in the Mood for Love"	32	AABA	6	6	11	6	none	15
"The Sweetest Sounds"	40	ABACt	4	7	6	9	4	15
"Ol' Man River"	32	AABA	7	9	7	8	none	16
"Body and Soul"	32	AABA	7	9	9	8	none	17
"I've Got a Crush on You"	32	ABAC	6	8	6	9	none	20
"Have Yourself a Merry Little Christmas"	32	AABA	7	9	12	10	none	21
"Tea for Two"	32	ABAC	6	7	6	11	none	21
"The Man I Love"	32	AABA	9	11	8	9	none	21
"They Didn't Believe Me"	32	ABCD	6	12	10	8	none	21
"Long Ago (and Far Away)"	32	ABAC	10	11	10	10	none	22
"You Are for Loving"	36	ABACt	7	11	7	11	5	24
"When Sunny Gets Blue"	36	AABAt	13	12	10	10	5	26
"Autumn in New York"	32	ABCD	9	10	11	10	none	29

Chart Explanations

1. Total number of chords includes all different chords. Many are used several times. For instance, C7 appears in two nonconsecutive bars of the "B" phrase in "I've Got a Crush on You." That chord is stated only once.

2. All chords are included, even though there are slight variations in some. For instance, Emin, Emin6, and Emin7 are employed in "You Are for Loving." They are properly listed here as three different chords.

3. Chords in each phrase are the number of different chords used in that section. Many are repeated in other phrases, but each phrase is listed separately. The number of chords under each phrase does not add up to the total number of chords in the song because of duplication.

4. Sheet music in the public library provided this information.

The statistics found in these twenty songs considered give us definite guidelines:

a. The number of chords in any given phrase is from three to thirteen, with eight being about the average.

b. Total number of chords in these songs is from eight to twenty-nine, averaging just under eighteen.

c. Twelve songs (60 percent) employed twenty chords or less.

d. Seventeen songs (85 percent) used twenty-two or fewer chords.

Why is there such a vast spread from eight to twenty-nine chords in a song? Does its form make a difference? We see that it definitely does.

The eight AABA songs analyzed contained between eight and twenty-one chords, averaging fourteen. You may wonder why there are that many in only sixteen bars of original music. Each "A" phrase is a repeat of eight (usually) bars of music, except that the final bar or so has some differences to lead into another phrase.

And you may ask this very legitimate question: If the melody line is virtually the same in every "A" phrase, aren't the chords identical in them?

Refer to the table just studied. Let's look at "I've Got a Crush on You." Each "A" phrase contains six chords. The initial full bar following the three eighth-note pickups of the first "A" phrase employs the B flat major 7 and A9 chords. In the second "A" of this

ABAC tune, the harmony is B flat major 7 and A7. We know that A9 and A7 are different chords, but they have a similar sound. There is no particular reason for not using either A9 or A7 in both measures of these paralleling "A" phrases—except that Messrs. Gershwin and Gershwin wanted it that way. And that is reason enough.

It seems logical that the ABAC form would use more chords than an AABA song because it contains twenty-four bars of original music—and it does employ more chords. The seven songs considered have from ten to twenty-four chords, with the average being about seventeen.

By the same reasoning, an ABCD song should—and does—require more chords. Each eight-bar phrase is not repeated; all thirty-two bars are original music. We analyzed two such songs. "They Didn't Believe Me" and "Autumn in New York" contain twenty-one and twenty-nine separate chords.

A tag ending may add a new chord or perhaps even several. We don't see any pronounced difference between tag and "non-tag" songs. The three songs with tags contained fifteen, twenty-four, and twenty-six separate chords. But the tag was not the significant reason for the larger number of chords.

Does the length of a song affect its total chord quantity? Not really. Fifteen of these twenty songs were thirty-two bars in length; they contained from eight to twenty-nine different chords. The forty-bar "The Sweetest Sounds" uses only fifteen chords. "This Is the Army, Mister Jones" is in 2/4 time. It has a march-time feel in its fifty-six bars, yet contains only nine separate chords.

A change of key at the bridge generally requires more chords. Four songs analyzed contain "B"—phrase key changes. Here are their total number of chords: "Body and Soul" (17); "Tea for Two" (21); "Long Ago (and Far Away)" (22); "When Sunny Gets Blue" (26).[3]

---

3. The sheet music on "Sunny" does not show an actual key change. However, its "B" harmony is so radically different from the "A" phrases in this AABA tune that it is a transposition for all practical purposes.

When is it necessary to change chords? Again we rely on the "ear" test. That simple examination will tell us:

1. When the current chord is not the best harmony to continue with, and a chord change will support the forthcoming melody better.
2. To resolve and lead into a series of different notes and other forthcoming chords in a natural-sounding fashion.
3. For a special effect, such as a melodic high point or climax.
4. To make the song prettier.

We can write songs, as our highly successful mentors have done, using from eight to twenty-nine different chords. Any place in that number seems to be safe harmonic ground. That 85 percent of these songs studied have twenty-two or less chords seems to be a good indicator.

How many chords is enough? About twenty-two, give or take a diminished, as long as they improve your song and sound good to you.

CHAPTER TWENTY-THREE

KEY SIGNATURE
or How Many Flats in Q Sharp?

As songwriters, we can write in twelve different keys. (If you want to be technical, there are really twice that number, since C sharp and D flat are two different keys, *et al.* But that hairsplitting isn't important here.) Hopefully, we are capable of using many of them—we won't use them all—and not just be "C key" songwriters.

If we want to sell songs, we had better *not* use every key. There are several time-proven reasons why we shouldn't.

Suppose Shirley goes to the music store to buy your latest top-of-the-chart hit. Her eyes brighten as she lifts the sheet music from the rack. She opens it with excitement, then frowns. Why? Because you wrote it in D flat. It might as well have been written in Indian sign language; she can't play in five flats.

Shirley would have bought your song had it been composed in keys she can handle: C, F, and G. Maybe she can also play in D, B flat, and perhaps E flat. Beyond those, she is either lost, or won't spend the effort at mastering what to her is a difficult key. After all, she wanted to play your song, not make a study project of it.

This age-old rule has been modified during the past two decades with the renewed popularity of the guitar. That instrument readily lends itself to playing in keys with sharps in their signatures. Earlier, a song written in A or E would have had the amateur musician put your music away and turn on the radio.

Since that "absolute" in key signatures has been altered, we have more latitude in writing. But the point remains: the simpler your key signature—meaning the fewer number of sharps and flats in it—the easier it is for most people to read. That translates quickly: more copies of your songs will be purchased.

Since you have versatility over the entire keyboard—or at least we hope you do—writing in a "Shirley" key is no hurdle. Maybe you wrote your song in D flat, because that key sounded best to you. Before you offer it for public applause, transpose it down a half step into C, or up a full step into E flat. Or if you composed in A flat, transpose it off a half step into G, or up a full step in B flat. That puts your song into a more musical common denominator; Shirley will take it home instead of looking for another tune in a key she can play.[1,2]

To answer the facetious question posed in this chapter's title, there are never any flats in a key with sharps in its signature, or vice versa. Here are the accidentals (meaning sharps or flats) in the various keys. This reference will be helpful to you for writing in (or ultimately transposing to) "Shirley" keys.

---

1. If you will pardon this personal confession, I can play in C, G, F, B flat, E flat, A flat, and D flat. With effort, I can perform in D and G flat. In other keys, I either fumble or am totally lost. If a singer requests the key of B, he/she gets a choice—either C or B flat—because he/she won't get much (nay, none!) accompaniment in B. Ditto a request in E; pick F or E flat.

Keep your song "closer to home" and you will find a larger following on the safer ground of more conventional keys.

2. Yes, different keys have different sounds. Our Conservatory students argued loud and long on this topic. But it is true. My explanation is a personal theory:

(a) The composer, familiar with his hands on the keyboard or guitar neck making certain harmonic sounds, gets an entirely different chord structure in an unfamiliar key. His lack of ability may keep him in simpler harmonies. (When composing a musical score, and the keys of E flat, F, B flat, C, and G begin to sound unimaginative, I go to less familiar keys: A flat, D flat, and G flat. I find new horizons, because they are relatively strange musical territory, and because I am less versatile there. I write a full lead sheet, delighted that I haven't become jaded, and transpose it to a more conventional key in which anybody can play.

(b) Some keys sound richer to compose in than others. Don't ask me why, but fact it is. Period.

Key	Number of Flats	Flatted Notes
C	none	none
F	1	B
B flat	2	B, E
E flat	3	B, E, A
A flat	4	B, E, A, D
D flat	5	B, E, A, D, G
G flat	6	B, E, A, D, G, C
C flat[3]	7	all

Key	Number of Sharps	Sharped Notes
C	none	none
G	1	F
D	2	F, C
A	3	F, C, G
E	4	F, C, G, D
B[3]	5	F, D, G, D, A
F sharp[4]	6	F, C, G, D, A, E
C sharp[5]	7	all

Another vital reason for choosing the correct key is the range of your song. (See chapter 24, "Song Range.") Remember our vocal limits. We can sing only so low and not too high; a span of ten or eleven notes is our maximum ability.

Let's take a hypothetical case. Suppose you are going to utilize that full range of eleven notes in a new song. Suppose, too, that you write in the key of C. And suppose further that the range is from A below middle C to the second D above middle C. You realize that you are on track; the key is simple (the simplest, in fact) and the range singable.

---

3. B natural has the same notes as the key of C flat.
4. F sharp has the same notes as the key of G flat.
5. C sharp has the same notes as the key of D flat.
The notes in these pairs of scales are *enharmonically* equivalent; that is, they sound the same but are written in a different way.

Let's take that same song and put it in the key of G. The total interval/span of notes doesn't change; it is still eleven. Now we are in trouble. The lowest note is E above middle C, and that is no problem. But the top note is the second A above middle C—the first line above the treble clef—and 90 percent (or is it 99 percent?) of the public can't sing that high.

Our "hypothetical" song is a true case—"Over the Rainbow." Harold Arlen and E. Y. Harburg wrote it into perpetuity by making certain that it met the rules. Its eleven-note range is singable by the public. (It won them an Academy Award in 1939 and our thankful applause ever since.)

Take a tip from the creators of that musical masterpiece; write in a key which Shirley can play and in a range for everybody in anybody's neighborhood to sing.

CHAPTER TWENTY-FOUR

SONG RANGE
or That Is a *High* Note!

By definition, range is "total distance between maximum limits." To put it in our lingo, range is "extreme intervals between the highest and lowest notes of a song."

There are two criteria which establish a song's range. We have mentioned both. The primary consideration is how high and low most people can sing. While that characteristic has a little variance, it is about a 10th or 11th. [1,2] Because of this compelling requirement, we will see that hit songwriters have conformed to these general boundaries in their songs.

The second reason is based on a performer's sight-reading ability. Any music reader knows every note from middle C (the first line below the treble clef) to the second A above middle C (the first line above the treble clef). Recognizing notes higher and lower

may be a problem. *Don't* compose up at that upper level. Most singers do not have vocal ability in that high atmosphere and can't read the notes even if they could reach them.

---

1. If you need a reminder on the explanation of these numbers, refer to chapter 20, "Chord Formation."

2. Singers have greater limits when performing before a live audience. The excitement—probably—gives them a two or three additional-note range.

These conclusions are easy to prove. Test them yourself. Sing the musical scale, starting on your lowest note—a tone you can hit in both vowel and consonant sounds with adequate volume. What is your total range? Unless you are exceptional, you will "top out" at about ten notes. Even if your range is unique (and you can sing through five octaves, as Yma Sumac astounded audiences in the 1950s), recognize your gift but write for the rest of us to sing.

Now study what your compatriots have composed. They adhered to these basic principles in their hit songs. Take a lesson from the following examples:

8th Range: "Rudolph the Red-Nosed Reindeer"; "The Christmas Song"; "Pennies from Heaven"; "The Hut Sut Song"; "Pagan Love Song."

9th Range: "White Christmas"; "Embraceable You"; "Peg o' My Heart"; "You Belong to Me"; "Once in a While"; "Deep in the Heart of Texas"; "Sentimental Journey"; "Moonlight Becomes You"; "Thanks for the Memory"; "I'm in the Mood for Love"; "Laura."

10th Range: "Small Hotel"; "Day by Day"; "Easter Parade"; "Tea for Two"; "Stardust"; "Too Young"; "You'll Never Know"; "Don't Fence Me In"; "Dream"; "East of the Sun"; "These Foolish Things"; "Mairzy Doats"; "It's Magic"; "Paper Doll."

11th Range: "Night and Day"; "Candy"; "Over the Rainbow"; "Did I Remember?"; "Maybe"; "Chattanooga Choo-Choo."

12th Range: "Indian Summer"; "All the Things You Are."

Two more standards set the optimum limits. "Now Is the Hour" has a 6th range, while "Deep Purple" has a fourteen-note span.

To put our art back into a scientific framework, look at these statistics:

Range	Number of Songs	Percentage
6th	1	2.5
8th	5	12.5
9th	11	27.5
10th	14	35.0
11th	6	15.0
12th	2	5.0
14th	1	2.5

The mode is a 10th range, with fourteen (35 percent) of these forty songs being in this note-span spread. Eleven tunes have a 9th range and comprise 27.5 percent of all songs analyzed here. Of even more importance are these significant numbers: 77.5 percent had a range of a 10th or less, and 92.5 percent of them employed a total interval of an 11th or less.

And that, fellow songwriters, tells us all we need to know about song range limits.

Composers of hit songs stay within a vocal range which Republicans, Baptists, army veterans, single girls, Rotarians, Ford owners, baseball fans, high school graduates, city dwellers, non-smokers, left-handed people, redheads, taxi drivers, dog lovers, (have we missed *any*body?), and all others can sing!

G. THAT FOOT-TAPPING SOUND

CHAPTER TWENTY-FIVE

TIME VALUES
or How Do I Score a Half Note, and When Do I Use It?

Dear Sir:

I have a problem. In the opening bar of my song entitled "I Think I Love You, More or Less, Maybe, and Perhaps," the first note is a dotted something-or-other, tied to something else. It is followed by a little longer note, then goes to what appears to be about a two-thirds note (give or take a few beats), and a string of quickies, which I can't make out because of an oil stain on my chart. Will that work?

Hit Song Writer

Dear Hit:

You missed! Pay a right-now visit to your library for a book on musical composition. You will find that almost anything goes in time values. Your song has proved to be the exception.

Sir

P.S. You should see your oculist, take a refresher course in grade school mathematics, and keep your manuscript out from under your car!

This far-fetched example is probably the *only* rhythmical array (or disarray) of notes with varying time values which cannot be utilized in a song. Nearly anything will, has, and does. We have applauded songs whose infinite variety of time-notes made them artistic and financial successes.

In our Conservatory class, we studied this subject as we did "writing" for students who could not put their notes on manuscript paper. (See chapter 2 " 'Write' the Songs You Write.") The first lesson was to have all neophyte composers tap their feet in 4/4 meter (this is important in every song we write; get a rhythmic beat as a frame of rhythm reference before starting). Then we played the first two bars of the classic, "White Christmas." On plain paper, they made marks which showed that the first note occupied the entire opening measure, and illustrated the four one-beat quarter notes in the second bar.

The great "All the Things You Are" was our next exercise. Students found that it also had a whole note in the first bar, and three counts and one count on the two notes in the second bar. We found more progress by each student.

Advancing through several other songs, we arrived at the masterful bridge in "Over the Rainbow." They discovered that there were eight notes with only four counts in a measure. By his own method, each student was beginning to understand proper time formations.

We then introduced them to a whole note (𝅝), half note (𝅗𝅥), quarter note (𝅘𝅥), and eighth note (𝅘𝅥𝅮). They learned that a dot behind any note increases its time value by half of the note it follows; for instance, the two-count half note gets three beats if it is a dotted half note (𝅗𝅥.). We stated that some notes are tied (𝅘𝅥𝅘𝅥), so that its sound is sustained into the next measure without being struck again. We spoke of triplets (𝅘𝅥𝅘𝅥𝅘𝅥³) or (³𝅘𝅥𝅮𝅘𝅥𝅮𝅘𝅥𝅮). That subject might as well have been Greek until we put it into a modern idiom of "three for the price of two": three quarter notes get two counts, and three eighth notes get one count if they are triplets.

Would that we could say that all hands became instant authorities. Our results ranged from innocent ignorance to mass confusion . . . until more explanation and additional practice sessions made slow-but-sure progress. Sooner or later—and mostly later— each student learned to score note-time values in his songs.

If this "time" area is new to you, these examples may be of help. Only two more rules are important for your basic understanding of the entire time framework:

1. In any time signature (be it 4/4, 3/4, 2/4, 6/8, or other) the first/top number shows the number of counts in each measure.
2. The bottom/second number shows what type of note always gets one count: a quarter note.

To further illustrate, in 4/4 time there are four beats to a bar, and a quarter note (𝅘𝅥) gets one count. In 3/4, or waltz, time there are three beats to a measure, and a quarter note gets one count.

Follow the suggestion stated in the "letter" which started this chapter. Study the many available texts at your library. They will have more detailed information.

Since probably 90 percent of our writing will be in 4/4 time (and the remainder in 3/4 meter), we did not go into detail on 2/4 and 6/8 time. Your library sources can explain them further. Other time signatures will also be illustrated, although they are never employed in popular music.

Learn more about this subject. Be an independent composer who can score your own material and place the correct time values on your notes.

Now that you know how to write note/time values, let's see what the pros use.

Throughout our treatise we have listed the ingredients which hit songs have in common, those statistical requirements. Are there any such time-pattern rules? Which combinations appear in the first measure of a song? Then what generally follows in the second bar? Does any survey show that a quarter note should lead into a half note, or vice versa, or other? Are triplets important? When are pickup notes employed?

The best answer to these questions is a study of examples. Look at the time-value patterns in the opening four bars of these thirty songs, all of which are in 4/4 time:

"What Is There to Say?"

"Everything Happens to Me"*

"Night and Day"*

"Candy"

"Tea for Two"

*These songs have pickup note(s) before the initial "A" phrase.

127

"Moonlight Becomes You"

"Have Yourself a Merry Little Christmas"

"Stardust"*

"Polka-Dots and Moonbeams"

"Rudolph the Red-Nosed Reindeer"

"Moonlight in Vermont"

"Lover"

"My Ideal"

"You Are My Sunshine"*

"Pennies from Heaven"

"Small Hotel"

"September Song"*

"September in the Rain"*

"How Long Has This Been Going On?"

"Thanks for the Memory"

"Hello, Dolly!"*

"Body and Soul"

"Sentimental Journey"

"I Took a Trip on a Train"

"Chattanooga Choo-Choo"

"Easter Parade"

"The Hut Sut Song"*

"Day by Day"

"Surrey with the Fringe on Top"

"You Are for Loving"

Let's check "the numbers game" to determine what, if any, rules prevail here. We find this prevalence:

Measure	Time Value Notes	Number of Songs Utilizing	Number of Songs Not
1st	♩ ♩ ♩ ♩	6	24
	♩. ♪ ♩. ♪	3	27
	♩ ♩	4	26
	𝅝	2	28

Measure	Time Value Notes	Number of Songs Utilizing	Number of Songs Not
2nd	𝅝 (whole note)	2	28
	♩ ♩ ♩ ♩	5	25
	♩ ♩ 𝅗𝅥	4	26
	♩ 𝅗𝅥.	3	27
3rd	𝅝 (whole note)	1	29
	𝅗𝅥 𝅗𝅥	4	26
	♩ ♩ ♩ ♩	10	20
4th	𝅝 (whole note)	6	24
	𝅗𝅥. ♩	3	27
	♩ ♩ ♩ ♩	6	24
	♩ ♫ ♩ ♩	2	28

In every other area, we found that the majority of songs conform to some particular pattern and design. That is not the case in time dimensions. We see that quarter notes are more frequently used in the opening four bars in the "A" phrase than other notes. We also see that a whole note predominates in the fourth bar. (It tends to "punctuate" the first half of that eight-bar "A" by ending a full lyrical sentence or establishing the song-plot subject.)

The principle found in these examples is a rule of minorities rather than majorities which were present in other content categories. Our conclusion, therefore, is simple: your time-value pattern has few restrictions.

What is the value of pickup notes? Are they important? In reviewing these songs, the answer is yes.

You will notice that eight of the thirty songs have pickup notes; they are used in 27 percent of them. More often, they were absent; twenty-two songs (or 73 percent) did not contain them. Three of those eight songs with pickup notes had only one note, two had two notes, and three had three pickup notes. In every case all are one-count quarter notes.

Lyrics tell us when to use them. If you have too many words in the opening lyric line to fit into the standard four-beat measure, pickup notes are required. The rule is that basic.

Only three of these thirty songs contained triplets. Are they important to us? Apparently so; 10 percent of those tunes utilized them. They offer us a different rhythmic flair from the conventional one-two-three-four-beat feel. Write them to give your song a slightly unusual and pleasant rhythm conception.

The dotted note is more often used than not. Our study shows that seventeen, or 56 percent, of these songs contained it. It can provide a syncopated sound in a tune, giving an exciting feel to its rhythm.

The use of tied notes is a well-accepted practice. Five of the songs considered employed this convention once, and five additional songs used it twice in their first four bars.

What is the musical rest? It appears in a song where no note is struck, and is exactly what its definition tells us: the music rests. How important is it? Obviously not as vital as notes, or every song would be the melody you now hear—none! But still rests can be well employed.

Here are music rests, in 4/4 time, and how they are illustrated on the musical staff:

1. A *whole* rest of four counts:

2. A *half* rest of two counts:

3. A *quarter* rest of one count:

4. An *eighth* rest of a half count:

In these thirty songs, only one contained a rest. That infrequency is not indicative of its importance. Use the rest to provide variety and color to your melody.

What does this study tell us? We repeat: Any combination of time-value notes will, has, and does work in hit songs. Almost without restriction, you can employ *any* number of notes in *any* bar of your song, as long as they add up to a total beat count of four. While bridges were not specifically spelled out here, that same "non-pattern" prevailed for the "B" phrase as it did in "A" sections.

Let us put the statement "any number of notes" into a little more definitive framework. In every bar, the maximum number of notes is eight. Eight eighth notes in 4/4 time is our optimum total. Popular songs are rarely written with shorter notes, such as sixteenths or thirty-seconds. Twenty-one of the thirty songs considered here, or 70 percent, have eighth notes in their initial phrases.

Use any note-time-value combinations you wish. Be guided by these observations and enjoy "time freedom" in your compositions.

CHAPTER TWENTY-SIX

RHYTHM
or A Cha-Cha Ain't One-Two-Three, Baby!

What rhythm will you use for your new tune? There are several options. On second thought, you probably don't have any if you have started to compose. Your song, as you heard while writing it, has made that decision for you. How? Simply.....

As you wrote the melody or the lyrics, a rhythm pattern seemed to come naturally for it. Your song easily took one of several directions. You beat your foot in time to its meter. It had either a three-beat emphasis or a four-beat feel. Those are the two predominant rhythms, of which there are several delineations. Let us take up three-quarter time first.

This is waltz time. Its essential beat is *one*-two-three, *one*-two-three. Note the stress on the *one* beat. That beat is accented in every bar. We know that each measure contains three counts and a quarter note gets one beat.

If your song still has not "told" you what rhythm form prevails, check and see if it falls naturally into this *one*-two-three format. Remember the last time you saw a conductor lead a chorus or orchestra in a waltz? His baton made a triangle in the air. He started high, coming downward to his right, and arrived there on the exact beat for the count of *one*. Then his baton came across his body horizontally to his left, and arrived there exactly on the *two* beat. He returned to his starting point upward on a diagonal line, arriving there on the count of *three*. This triangle is a natural for a musical director to use because it emphasizes the *one*-two-three beats of the 3/4 time.

This rhythm pattern will be employed in a medium or slow tempo. Examples of songs using 3/4 time are "The Sweetheart of Sigma Chi"; "The Missouri Waltz"; "The Anniversary Waltz"; "My Buddy"; "The Boy Next Door"; "Together"; "Always"; "The

Tennessee Waltz"; "The Waltz You Saved for Me"; "When I Grow Too Old to Dream"; "Are You Lonesome Tonight?"; "Let Me Call You Sweetheart"; "What the World Needs Now Is Love"; "Fascination"; "Let's Take an Old-Fashioned Walk."

There is also a fast waltz. It has the same flavor but it is not in 3/4 time. This rhythm is 6/8 time, with six beats to a measure in which an eighth note gets one count. It cuts in half the usual note values, while doubling the number of bars of the song. Its best examples are "The Air Force Song"; "Oh, Mama"; "Buckle Down, Winsocki"; and Victor Herbert's "Toyland." Its use is rare, and hit songs in this rhythm have been few.

The difference in both of these three-beat feel songs is not a hair-splitting technicality. Each is a true rhythm category. However, if you are in doubt as to whether it is 3/4 or 6/8 time, write your song in 3/4 time. Then in the upper left-hand corner make the notation "upbeat." A performer will understand your suggestion and render it as you intended.

Those hints should help you to determine if your song is in 3/4 or 6/8 time. There aren't many of either. The best test of all of the things which a waltz is *not*, the characteristics belonging to 4/4 time.

Probably 98 percent[1] of all popular songs are in 4/4 meter. Its rhythm feel is as easy to recognize as the 3/4 time tune.

The first test, obviously, is that it does not fit into the *one*-two-three beat category. It naturally calls for a foot-tapping one-two-three-four pattern.

If you have determined that 4/4 time is your rhythm form, you face another decision. Perhaps, again, your song "told" you what variation of 4/4 time to employ. Is it slow or medium tempo or is it upbeat?

---

1. Not quite. "Your Hit Parade" survey shows that eleven of 332 weekly top favorite songs were written in 3/4 time. That is 3.3 percent of the total; 96.7 percent had 4/4 meter.

The melody isn't the only factor in making this decision. The lyric message can also be important.

Virtually all negative lyrics are essentially slow. Examples are "Ev'ry Time"; "You Are for Loving"; "Ghost of a Chance"; "There's No You"; "Cottage for Sale"; "Ev'rything Happens to Me."

With few exceptions, minor-key songs are in slow tempo. That rhythm accentuates the "blue" mood of a lyric story. Examples are "Gloomy Sunday" and "Summertime."

Philosophical songs are written in slow tempo. A faster rhythm does not lend itself to the pronounced message which the composer/lyricist is making for two reasons: It needs longer notes on which to get the lyrical point across, and the upbeat feel would destroy its serious statement and content. Examples are "Climb Every Mountain"; "If"; "The Impossible Dream"; "You'll Never Walk Alone"; "Ol' Man River."

The twelve-bar "blues" progression can go either way. If you write in that chord progression, it can be slow or fast or medium in tempo. Let your lyrics help establish your pace.

Most standard love songs belong to the danceable medium-tempo category. Examples are "Stardust"; "All the Things You Are"; "Moonlight in Vermont"; "Embraceable You"; "Stars Fell on Alabama."

The older and perennial jazz-type songs are upbeat. Their lyric messages are affirmative. Examples include "Tea for Two"; "September in the Rain"; "Chattanooga Choo-Choo"; "Pennies from Heaven"; "How High the Moon"; "Mountain Greenery"; "Ja-Da."

We have considered the wide scope of the 4/4 time performed in slow, medium, or "swing it" tempos. Other 4/4 rhythm forms are worth your consideration. Some are slightly more sophisticated. They have important differences which should be recognized.

"Latin" covers a broad area. It has a tricky sound, a rhythmic let's-dance appeal. An interjecting emphatic off-beat is definitely *not* the straight one-two-three-four feel.[2] It can suggest a South American setting, provide a mysterious air, or add a haunting mood to your melody. It is especially important in providing variety in a musical theatre score.

Latin sounds include rhumba, tango, beguine, conga, cha-cha, calypso, and bossa nova. Each has that lively, magnetic feeling. They all belong to the same rhythmic family, but they have slight differences, making them no closer than "cousins" in their relationship. We won't delve into those variations; your library will offer detailed data on them. Examples are "Green Eyes"; "Amapola"; "Frenesi"; "Tico-Tico"; "Begin the Beguine"; "Mama Inez"; "Hernando's Hideaway"; "Rum and Coca-Cola"; "My Shawl" (by the master of Latin bandleaders, Xavier Cugat); "The Girl from Ipanima."

We mentioned that most minor-key songs are essentially slow in tempo. A few are in the Latin category. If the original intent of the composer was not to perform it with the Latin feel, most renditions of these songs adopt it. Why? It seems to "fit." Examples are "Get Out of Town" and "You'd Be So Nice to Come Home To."

Marches have the four-beat feel. More often than not, however, they are written 2/4. That rhythm is split-time, similar to changing the 3/4 waltz into 6/8 meter. It is faster, cutting the note values in what would be 4/4 time in half while doubling the total number of bars. Examples are "This Is the Army, Mister Jones"; Seventy-Six Trombones"; "The New Ashmolean Marching Society and Students Conservatory Band"; plus the standard marches and college fight songs.

---

2. In our Songwriting class, a student performed his new song that had a Latin beat. Immediately he had the enthusiastic attention of every member and their excited affirmative response.

Why? Yes, it was a good tune. More than that, it was the first song demonstrated in class with a Latin rhythm. It was fresh, unique, and different.

A Latin rhythm can give your songs an appeal because it isn't the conventional and standard 4/4 beat. Use it to your advantage.

Another 2/4 time type is the polka. It is lively and spirited. If a march sounds like "hup! two! hup! two!" in a strictly-structured military pattern, the polka may have pickup notes, a less regimented melody, is more free-flowing, bouncy, and happier.

The polka has the "oom-pah" echo of the old beer-garden brass band. It came to America from Germany, Poland, the Balkan countries, and the southern Slavik regions. It remains popular in those ethnic communities. Its best examples are "The Beer Barrel Polka" and "The Pennsylvania Polka."

Not all 2/4-time tunes are marches or polkas. Some few are more conventional. They might well have been written in 4/4 time. Why weren't they? Our best guess is that the composer felt that his song sounded better in 2/4 time. Examples are Richard Rodgers' "The Sweetest Sounds" and the Gershwin "I've Got a Crush on You."

Are there any other rhythm categories? Yes, rubato. This Latin word means "without rhythm." You read it correctly—*without* rhythm. How can a song have no beat at all? Before we point out the single rare specimen, this may refresh your memory.

You have heard a performer sing a song through, then return to perform the verse without any beat. It provides a unique approach which is interesting to hear. (See chapter 16, "The Verse.") You may still be doubtful; virtually all of that type of rendition had a regular beat through most of the tune. But can an *entire* song be totally void of rhythm?

One song did—"Nature Boy." Nat "King" Cole recorded this eden ahbez (the composer never used capital letters) number in 1948. It was a big hit. But this example is so rare—the only song of its rhythm (or non-rhythm) pattern of the several hundred tunes considered here—that it is not a practical form to follow.

In the same non-practical discipline is another unique rhythm: 5/4 time. As you can see, it has five quarter notes in each measure. Its sole example to make any musical splash was Marilyn Maye's outstanding recording of "Take Five," an upbeat tune. Opera composers employ this rhythm along with other meters such as 7/4, 9/4, and beyond. They are mentioned here for your additional knowledge. With that single exception, there are no songs which have received any following in these far-out tempos. As popular songwriters, we can be sure that they are not for us.

We repeat: Nearly every time your song will decide for you what its rhythm will be. Accept its answer because of its natural "feel." Most of your compositions will be in 4/4 time. Once that basic pattern is established, its lyrical message will dictate whether it has a slow, medium, or fast tempo. You can also tell if it has the persuasive flavor of Latin, the strict demands of a march, or the bouncy beat of a polka. The 3/4-beat of a waltz is so compellingly different that it is difficult to miss.

Compose in 4/4 time and you won't go wrong. Use 3/4 rhythm for that rare song which easily falls into the "triangle."

Listen to your song as you write it. It will tell you what rhythm to use.

H. LEST WE FORGET

CHAPTER TWENTY-SEVEN

WRITING A MUSICAL STAGE SCORE
or Oklahoma! Here I come!

"I'm a songwriter, not a score-writer," may be your immediate comment. As a quick and emphatic afterthought you might add, "and I'm for sure not a playwright!" Okay. At least, not yet. Neither was anybody else... until we wrote our first score or play. So read along and keep an open mind while we discuss this new territory. You may be enjoyably surprised and excited.

Along with jazz, the musical comedy is a true American art form. We didn't inherit it from the European concert halls as we did the opera and operetta. Yes, the argument can be made that it is an outgrowth of them. But it matured, was refined, and further developed. It has since been borrowed from us, adopted and adapted around the world. It bears the "made in USA" creative stamp. We have every right to be proud. Many of us should be a part of it, and we can be.

The musical stage is no longer the sole eminent domain of comedy. While it went through that syndrome, it has widened to include every musical and dramatic emotion.

Let's take a look at that process. These plays and their dates are important in this evolution...

1927: Jerome Kern and Oscar Hammerstein II broadened its scope with *Showboat*. This was the first real breakthrough from the slim-plotted musical comedies preceding it. It is interesting to note that both the composer and lyricist called it "a musical comedy," probably because that was the best description in public use at that time.

1943: Hammerstein and Richard Rodgers trekked in a new and different creative direction from the conventional musical with *Oklahoma!* And what a difference! It had a ballet, psychopath, murder, and no chorus line. Some called it a "folk opera"; others termed it "a play with music." By any definition, a musical comedy it wasn't. By every definition, a stage classic it is!

1943: Hammerstein was again the inventive iconoclast with his modernization of Bizet's opera *Carmen*. With his up-to-date treatment, it became *Carmen Jones*. A critic called it "a memorable milestone in the onward course of the great American showshop." Semantics notwithstanding, this was a musical drama or, more probably, a musical tragedy.

Those were the turning points which brought the musical stage from its narrow and singular viewpoint of tuneful comedy to the same full emotional range which the straight play (a play without music) has enjoyed.

Others followed, showing that these three productions were neither experimental nor accidental musical plays. Rodgers and Hammerstein continued their departure with *Carousel*[1] in 1945, *Allegro* in 1947, *South Pacific* in 1949, *The King and I* and *Pipe Dream* in 1951.

Nor were these gentlemen the only contributors to the wider scope of music in the theater. *Lost in the Stars*, which composer Kurt Weill termed "a musical tragedy," was first staged at the Music Box Theatre in New York on October 30, 1949. Leonard Bernstein's *West Side Story*, opening at New York's Winter Garden

---

1. If legend be true, the internationally renowned Italian opera composer, Giacomo Puccini, wrote Ferenc Molnár, the Hungarian author of *Liliom*, requesting permission to adapt his classic story into an opera. No, was Molnár's reply. Instead, he accepted the offer of Rodgers and Hammerstein, the American deans of the musical stage, to use it in that discipline. Such was the tribute to these creators and our art form, now horizon-wide in emotional dimension, which could best portray his outstanding work.

Liliom became *Carousel* in 1945 to thrill millions of theatergoers and music lovers ever since.

Theater on September 26, 1957, is a theatrical standard. It is a musical tragedy by plot definition, a musical triumph in terms of perennial success.

Enough of history. If you are still negative-minded about your participation as a writer/composer/lyricist for the musical stage, stay with us. These experiences may prove that this creative field is not impossible for you.

We gave this assignment to our Conservatory class: Write a song at each of the five complication/conflict/crisis points in a basic plot. For lack of a better title, we called it "Boy Meets Girl." No dialogue was required, but a story-line explanation by each new playwright/composer was needed to lead up to the conflicts. Only two characters were allowed; therefore, either Boy, Girl, or both of them sang all songs.

The plot was purposely elementary. We had strong conflict events which were the following:

1. Boy meets Girl; they like each other, plan a date.
2. Boy stands Girl up; she is mad.
3. Girl gives Boy another chance; all is forgiven.
4. Boy breaks date; Girl is angry when she sees Boy out with another girl (who is his cousin, but Girl doesn't know it).
5. Girl is irate. Boy apologizes, explains, and tells her that he can't live without her. She forgives him, feels the same way, and they live happily ever after.

If the plot was simple, it was a major undertaking for single-song composers. We were amazed at the fine efforts these young instant playwrights produced.

When the assignment was announced, one student stated that he had no interest in musical theater; he was in the class to learn to write songs unrelated to a story. Two days later he called, apologizing for his terse negative pronouncement. The following week he performed five well-constructed songs, all of them plot-involved, to the enjoyment and applause of the class. Then he said that this was the most interesting assignment he had ever been given; it opened his eyes to a new musical horizon which he had never before considered.

Let that challenge be an inspiration for you. As an exercise, you might want to complete this same assignment which motivated these students toward a fresh and exciting musical area for them.

What does music do for the stage? It must fulfill one or more of four definite objectives:

1. Bring a new and different *element of entertainment*, adding to the action between characters.
2. *Further the plot*, stating in lyrics what would otherwise be dialogue to move the play into complications, conflicts, a crisis, and its ultimate conclusion.
3. *Know the characters*, developing them for a better understanding.
4. *"Frolic,"* providing nothing more than audience pleasure. This type of song could be easily omitted from a score. It is not essential to the play.

On the professional stage with pre-Broadway tryouts on the road (historically Boston, New Haven, Hartford, or Philadelphia; more recently, Washington is the predominant location), the decision is made to keep or strike a "frolic" song, based on audience response. "Ol' Man River" is an excellent example. Can you imagine *Show Boat* without this great song?

Music on stage isn't just a fill-in frill. It is an important essential toward the full development and understanding of the story line and the characters in a play. And it entertains.

The number of songs in hit musical plays range from twelve in *1776* to twenty-six in *Hair*. An average seems to be about seventeen, with three-plus reprises. A reprise provides the same advantage that repeating the title in a tune performs: the listener has another opportunity to hear and remember it.

The supreme test of a score is met if an audience can leave the theater humming or singing the melody of at least three tunes. This is easy on a perennial; anyone can emerge from the exciting experience of seeing *Best Foot Forward* today, being totally familiar with most of its stellar numbers which have been popular for nearly thirty-five years. But to do so on the first hearing, before the tunes have become popular standards, is to pronounce "success" for its composers.

Writing a score requires real talent. We can easily write one tune, give it our best effort, know that we have written—and rewritten—an outstanding song, and quit; that single song is our current goal. The composition of a score demands real creative ability plus a critical look at the seventeen-or-so tunes we have composed. Do any of them sound like our other songs in the same play? Is there a general similarity? Chances are definitely yes. But you can avert this strong possibility with a log/chart/work sheet on the specifics of each song.

I always find this tool very helpful, as in my score for *Treasure Island*. This Robert Louis Stevenson classic has every essential to become an outstanding musical: it is an exciting drama, it has an "all-family" plot, it is known by every American over the age of twelve, and its familiarity needs no major promotional activity to excite the public.

To keep it from sounding stereotyped in its nineteen-song score, this chart was developed. Each category was a reminder to divorce every song in every possible way from every other tune. It is recommended to you.

MUSICAL PLAY WORK SHEET

Page	Act	Scene	Song	Singer(s)	Form	Mood	Tempo-Rhythm	Rhyme Words	Comments
5	I	1	"Go to Sea Once More"	Sailors	ABABAB	Chanty/Maritime	Medium upbeat, strong 4/4 feel	"then/again; more/before"	With spirit; split time last 4 bars
9	I	2	"Goodbye, Jim, Goodbye"	Mrs. Hawkins	AABAt	Philosophical	Medium, 3/4	"goodbye/high; yearn/return"	88 bars
17	I	3	"Never Marry a Sailor"	Barmaids	ABABABt	Lighthearted	Upbeat	"port/sport; sea/me"	Special. Transpose from E flat to F, G, each rendition; has "hey-nonny-nonny" turnaround between each AB section
27	I	4	"Lingo"	Long John Silver	ABABABt	Chanty/Maritime	Medium	"tall/wall; below/know; there/where; do/you"	Long John teaches Jim in pleasant mood; Jim comments briefly during song.

There are many advantages which this work sheet provides. At a glance we can tell how many *pages* come between each musical number for good song spacing. (As a general rule, a non-song page takes slightly less than a minute of stage performance time.) It indicates *act* and *scene*, keeping us from placing too many songs in one scene and from omitting music in others. The *singer(s)* category warns us against several consecutive chorus numbers followed by back-to-back solos or vice versa. *Form, mood, tempo/rhythm, rhyme words* provide the same "scorecard" so that no duplicate type follows another. *Comments* give us additional benchmarks with which to assure variety in our score.

You will notice that some other items which belong on our work sheet (as discussed in chapter 3, "Tools") are absent. We have used that item on each song as it is written regarding *title placement, title words, title repeat, number of words, range, key signature*, et al.

This work sheet is a valuable help for this special-purpose area of composition. You will find it important in writing your musical play score.

If you just gave up the idea because of the quantity of musical composition involved (yes, it does take hours at the piano and typewriter), wait a minute. Think of the thrill which this challenge offers—writing a complete score that develops characters and moves the story line and entertains. Imagine the self-induced obligation—having to produce some seventeen songs—and your satisfaction in its accomplishment. Consider the joy—joining the great musical stage contributors who have added to this unique American cultural form. Experience fame and fortune when your play achieves success.

In addition to the thrilling fringe benefits, many theatrical composers have found a pot of gold at the end of the theater's rainbow. Long after the final curtain has been rung down and an excited audience leaves its seats, they will remember the songs they applauded. And they will enjoy them again in later productions, records, perhaps a film version of the play, and as the man on the street whistling them.

Here is a too-brief list of hit songs that had their origins on the musical stage. . . .

Year	Tune	Show	Composer/Lyricist
1926	"The Birth of the Blues"	*George White's Scandals*	DeSylva, Brown, Henderson
	"The Desert Song"	*The Desert Song*	Harbach and Hammerstein
	"The Blue Room"	*The Girl Friend*	Rodgers and Hart
1927	"Ol' Man River"	*Show Boat*	Hammerstein and Kern
	"The Best Things in Life Are Free"	*Good News*	DeSylva, Brown, Henderson
1928	"Stout-Hearted Men"	*The New Moon*	Hammerstein and Romberg
	"How Long Has This Been Going On"	*Rosalie*	Gershwin and Gershwin
1929	"With a Song in My Heart"	*Spring Is Here*	Rodgers and Hart
	"Zigeuner"	*Bittersweet*	Coward
1930	"Body and Soul"	*Three's a Crowd*	Heyman and Green
	"Embraceable You"	*Girl Crazy*	Gershwin and Gershwin
	"Fine and Dandy"	*Fine and Dandy*	Jones and Swift
1931	"Dancing in the Dark"	*The Band Wagon*	Dietz and Schwartz
1932	"April in Paris"	*Walk a Little Faster*	Harburg and Duke
	"Night and Day"	*The Gay Divorcé*	Porter
	"The Song Is You"	*Music in the Air*	Hammerstein and Kern
1933	"Easter Parade"	*As Thousands Cheer*	Berlin
	"Smoke Gets in Your Eyes"	*Roberta*	Harbach and Kern
	"Yesterdays"	*Roberta*	Harbach and Kern

Year	Tune	Show	Composer/Lyricist
1934	"All Through the Night"	*Anything Goes*	Porter
	"I Get a Kick Out of You"	*Anything Goes*	Porter
	"Anything Goes"	*Anything Goes*	Porter
	"You and the Night and the Music"	*Revenge with Music*	Dietz and Schwartz
1935	"Begin the Beguine"	*Jubilee*	Porter
	"East of the Sun"	*Stags at Bay*	Brooks Bowman
	"It Ain't Necessarily So"	*Porgy and Bess*	Gershwin and Gershwin
	"My Romance"	*Jumbo*	Rodgers and Hart
	"Summertime"	*Porgy and Bess*	Heyward and Gershwin
1936	"I Can't Get Started"	*Ziegfeld Follies*	Gershwin and Duke
	"Its D'Lovely"	*Red, Hot and Blue*	Porter
	"Small Hotel"	*On Your Toes*	Rodgers and Hart
1937	"The Lady Is a Tramp"	*Babes in Arms*	Rodgers and Hart
	"My Funny Valentine"	*Babes in Arms*	Rodgers and Hart
1938	"Get Out of Town"	*Leave It to Me*	Porter
	"I Married an Angel"	*I Married an Angel*	Rodgers and Hart
	"September Song"	*Knickerbocker Holiday*	Anderson and Weill
1939	"All the Things You Are"	*Very Warm for May*	Hammerstein and Kern
1940	"How High the Moon"	*Two for the Show*	Hamilton and Lewis
	"Bewitched"	*Pal Joey*	Rodgers and Hart

147

Year	Tune	Show	Composer/Lyricist
1941	"Buckle Down, Winsocki"	*Best Foot Forward*	Martin and Blane
1942	"This Is the Army, Mister Jones"	*This Is the Army*	Berlin
1943	"Oklahoma!"	*Oklahoma!*	Rodgers and Hammerstein
	"Speak Low"	*One Touch of Venice*	Nash and Weill
1944	"Right as the Rain"	*Bloomer Girl*	Arlen and Harburg
1945	"Close as Pages in a Book"	*Up in Central Park*	Fields and Romburg
	"If I Loved You"	*Carousel*	Rodgers and Hammerstein
1946	"There's No Business Like Show Business"	*Annie Get Your Gun*	Berlin
1947	"How Are Things in Glocca Morra?"	*Finian's Rainbow*	Harburg and Lane
	"Almost Like Being in Love"	*Brigadoon*	Lerner and Loewe
	"A Fellow Needs a Girl"	*Allegro*	Rodgers and Hammerstein
1948	"Once in Love with Amy"	*Where's Charley?*	Loesser
	"So in Love"	*Kiss Me, Kate*	Porter
1949	"Some Enchanted Evening"	*South Pacific*	Rodgers and Hammerstein
	"Diamonds Are a Girl's Best Friend"	*Gentlemen Prefer Blondes*	Robin
	"Let's Take an Old-Fashioned Walk"	*Miss Liberty*	Berlin
1950	"It's a Lovely Day Today"	*Call Me Madam*	Berlin
	"A Bushel and a Peck"	*Guys and Dolls*	Loesser

Year	Tune	Show	Composer/Lyricist
1951	"I Whistle a Happy Tune"	King and I	Rodgers and Hammerstein
	"I Talk to the Trees"	Paint Your Wagon	Lerner and Loewe
1952	"Wish You Were Here"	Wish You Were Here	Rome
1953	"Baubles, Bangles and Beads"	Kismet	Wright, Forrest, and Borodin
	"Ohio"	Wonderful Town	Bernstein, Comden, and Green
	"I Love Paris"	Can-Can	Porter
1954	"Fanny"	Fanny	Rome
	"Small Talk"	The Pajama Game	Adler and Ross
1955	"All of You"	Silk Stockings	Porter
	"Young and Foolish"	Plain and Fancy	Horwitt and Hague
	"You Gotta Have Heart"	Damn Yankees	Adler and Ross
1956	"Joey, Joey, Joey"	Most Happy Fella	Loesser
	"The Party's Over"	Bells Are Ringing	Comden and Green
	"On the Street Where You Live"	My Fair Lady	Lerner and Loewe
	"Mack the Knife"	The Threepenny Opera	Blitzstein and Weill
1957	"Maria"	West Side Story	Sondheim and Bernstein
	"Seventy-Six Trombones"	Music Man	Willson
1958	"I Enjoy Being a Girl"	Flower Drum Song	Rodgers and Hammerstein

Year	Tune	Show	Composer/Lyricist
1959	"People"	*Gypsy*	Sondheim and Styne
	"The Sound of Music"	*The Sound of Music*	Rodgers and Hammerstein
1960	"Soon It's Gonna Rain"	*The Fantasticks*	Schmidt and Jones
	"Camelot"	*Camelot*	Lerner and Loewe
	"Put On a Happy Face"	*Bye Bye Birdie*	Strouse and Adams
	"Hey, Look Me Over"	*Wildcat*	Leigh and Coleman
	"The Trolley Song"	*Meet Me in St. Louis*	Martin and Blane
1961	"I Believe in You"	*How to Succeed in Business Without Really Trying*	Loesser
1962	"What Kind of Fool Am I?"	*Stop the World*	Bricusse and Newley
1963	"As Long as He Needs Me"	*Oliver*	Bart
1964	"Hello Dolly!"	*Hello, Dolly!*	Herman
	"Sunrise, Sunset"	*Fiddler on the Roof*	Harnick and Bock
1965	"Who Can I Turn To?"	*The Roar of the Greasepaint—The Smell of the Crowd*	Bricusse and Newley
1966	"The Impossible Dream"	*Man of La Mancha*	Darion and Leigh
1967	"Cabaret"	*Cabaret*	Ebb and Kander
1968	"The Happy Time"	*Being Alive*	Ebb and Kander

Year	Tune	Show	Composer/Lyricist
1969	"Aquarius"	*Hair*	Rado and Ragni
	"I've Gotta Be Me"	*Golden Rainbow*	Marks
	"Yours, Yours, Yours"	*1776*	Stone and Edwards
1970	"Two by Two"	*Two by Two*	Rodgers and Charnin
1971	"Beautiful Girls"	*Follies*	Sondheim
1972	"We Go Together"	*Grease*	Jacobs and Casey
1973	"It's a Deal"	*Raisin*	Woldin and Brittan
1974	"Miss Lorelei Lee"	*Lorelei*	Styne and Robin
	"The Glamorous Life"	*A Little Night Music*	Sondheim
1975	"Music and the Mirror"	*A Chorus Line*	Hamlish and Kleban

If some songs from these more recent successful plays do not yet rival "Stardust" in terms of popularity, the fortunes of time have not had a chance to prove them as standards. However, they are important to their plays and are listed for that reason. We will await history's verdict while enjoying them.[2]

This is a great area of creative endeavor. If you can write one song, you can stretch your imaginative talent to fulfill the needs and opportunities awaiting you with a total score.

Answer the call of this rare and demanding challenge as successful theatrical composers have. And tell *Oklahoma!* to move over!

---

2. The managing director of Kansas City's Starlight Theatre received me and my musical comedy, *Somewhat Gray,* with lukewarm enthusiasm: "I don't want to be pessimistic. This may be a great show. But you are in the most competitive field in the world where there is little room at the top. Today, I would bet against a new play by Berlin, Porter, Rodgers, or any other leading composer because the odds would be with me. The chances of your *Somewhat Gray* being a hit are less than one in a hundred."

Those odds don't deter me, and don't let them discourage you. I continue to write for the musical stage. We know that our chances are slim. Just as long as there is room for one—only one—success, there is room for us. That "one" could very well be you.

CHAPTER TWENTY-EIGHT

COPYRIGHT YOUR SONG
or Be Safe Rather than Sorry

The lay public has a general misconception of protection provided by a copyright. They think that we are saved from plagiarism, inoculated against infringement, and are freed from song-rustlers invading our material. Such is not the case.

Copyrighting offers us a single safeguard. It proves that we are on record as having written a song on or before a specific date, and that no one can copy or print it without our permission. Just as its name implies, it protects the owner's exclusive "right to copy," which means his individual right to use. That is all it provides: nothing more, nothing less.

In 1976, President Gerald R. Ford signed Public Law # 94-553 to become effective on January 1, 1978. This is the first major revision of our copyright statutes since 1909. It is a welcome change, giving us immense benefits over the old law. It is the result of several decades of protestations by our fraternity for fairer economic treatment. It corresponds to the equitable terms which other countries have long afforded their musical creators.

This new law includes the following provisions as of January 1, 1978:

1. The term for a copyright will be the life of the composer plus fifty years. There will be no renewal term.
2. All songs copyrighted prior to that date will have a term of twenty-eight years, plus a renewal period of forty-seven years, for a total span of seventy-five years.
3. Renewals of songs copyrighted before that date must be obtained within a year prior to their original expiration date. As stated, a forty-seven-year renewal term will be granted.
4. Songs which are currently under a renewal term are extended

by law from 1976 to give a total of seventy-five years' protection. The composer need not apply for it.

5. In the event of collaboration, the life-plus-fifty-years applies to the final survivor of the co-composers.

6. Copyrights do not expire on their exact anniversary dates, but continue through December 31 of the year in which they would fall into the public domain.

7. Jukebox operators will pay a fee of $8.00 per jukebox. Cable television and public broadcasting will also be licensed and charged by the Copyright Royalty Tribunal, a new government agency which will set and review such fees.

8. An increase from 2¢ per song per record to 2.75¢ will be paid for sound recordings. That rate will also be regulated by the Copyright Royalty Tribunal.

These are the highlights of this highly beneficial (and, at last, equitable) law for songwriters. For additional information, a copy of the new law may be obtained from the Copyright Office, Library of Congress, Washington, D.C. 20559. If you belong to ASCAP, BMI, or AGAC, their offices have data for further assistance to you.

Acquiring a copyright is an easy procedure. Request a blank copyright application, Form PA, from the Copyright Office (there are four different copyright forms; be certain to specify Form PA, which is for Performing Arts only). It is available at no cost.

When you receive this application, do the following:

(a) **Complete Form PA. It is actually a double form which requires you to make a carbon copy.**

(b) Include one legible copy of your lead sheet. *Never* send the only copy you have.

(c) **Write a check payable to the Register of Copyrights for the required amount ($10.00 when this book was written).**

Your copyright, containing official dates and a registration number, will be sent to you within several weeks.

I have composed a simple all-business letter. I keep a copy of it for my records until the document Form PA is returned. All it needs is a date, song title, and a signature along with the three enclosures. Here it is . . . .

Register of Copyrights
Library of Congress
Washington, D. C. 20559

Dear Sir:

Please find the following items enclosed:

1) My original song, _____
2) **Completed Form PA.**
3) **My personal check in the amount of (fill in the amount)** ___.

Kindly grant the writer copyright privileges on the above material.

Thank you for your attention and cooperation.

Sincerely yours,

enclosures

A copyright legend must be placed on your lead sheet prior to forwarding it. This item customarily goes at the very bottom; should there not be space, place it visibly elsewhere on the front page. It needs this exact phraseology: Copyright © 1977 John Q. Doe (the year you apply for copyright and your name). Note the circle around the small "c". This provides further protection for your song with over sixty countries that belong to the Universal Copyright Convention which was established September 16, 1955.

What and when to copyright is a question only you can answer. We songwriters are guilty of copyrighting material—and spending $10.00—unnecessarily and too frequently.[1] **If you are keeping your song for your own pleasure without offering it to the public or publishers, you do not need copyright protection. If you are sending it to music companies, then it is probably best to copyright it.**

Note the word "probably." Should you forward your tune to a well-established publisher, that firm is above stealing it for two reasons: (1) Publishers know that they must pay royalties for every song published and cannot avoid that standard expense, and (2) they do not want a possible lawsuit from you.

However, in every case, you are safer with a registered copyright.

An often-asked question is: What protection do I have by mailing a copy of my song back to myself, either by registered or first class mail? The answer is, I don't know. To protect your material, your best security is a documented copyright.

A title cannot be copyrighted. There are probably a thousand songs entitled "I Love You," and many have official copyright registration.

---

1. I spent several hundred dollars for copyrights on songs which were never sent to publishers. I didn't need the protection, and it was a useless expense.

There are certain limitations to that rule. For instance, you could expect a court battle if you manufactured a car and called it "Ford" because the Ford car is a well-established name upon which you would be encroaching.[2]

Another frequently asked question by my Conservatory students is: How much of a song melody may be duplicated in another tune before it becomes an infringement? And how different must the time/note values be in the new song which has the same notes? Again, I do not know. Attorney Louis Nizer's book *My Life in Court* has an interesting chapter on this exact subject.

Look at these tunes which have sound-alike portions:

1. "How High the Moon" and "What Kind of Fool Am I?" have the same first five notes, although they are in different time values.
2. The first four notes are identical in "Begin the Beguine" and "Someone to Watch over Me," with contrasting time values.
3. "This Is Our Once-a-Year Day" (from *Pajama Game* by Adler and Ross), "Have Yourself a Merry Little Christmas" (the Blane and Martin standard from *Meet Me in St. Louis*),

---

2. I have had two such experiences. Harold Baker Lyon asked me to collaborate with him. It was about 1960 when the movie, *The World of Susie Wong* was being filmed. We wrote a song of the same title, hoping that the producers would use it to add a musical dimension to their publicity—and an increased monetary measure to our net worths. Forwarding it to them, we received a succinct reply from their legal counsel. They advised us that the producers were not interested, that we could not claim fame and fortune by hanging onto the coattails of this to-be-well-established movie, and to cease and desist or stand by for a legal broadside. We quietly ceased and desisted!

A second encounter regarded my original play, *Give 'Em Hell, Harry!* produced in May, 1970. When Sam Gallu's production of the same title with a one-man cast of James Whitmore arrived on the national scene in 1975, my lawyer contacted Gallu. His attorney's letter was courteous but definite: my play had achieved no widespread recognition, the title was a well-known phrase relating to President Truman, and there was also a book published in the 1950s with the same title. My counsel and I agreed that we had no legal grounds for objection and made none.

Incidentally, I was backstage with Whitmore after his magnificent portrayal of Will Rogers. During our conversation, you can bet that I did not bring up that subject!

and "Ballerina" (the 1947 hit by Bob Russell and Carl Sigman which bandleader/vocalist Vaughn Monroe's recording made famous) all share the identical opening four notes, varying them with different time values.

4. "The Christmas Song" and "Over the Rainbow" have three duplicate opening notes, but they differ in their time values.

5. "September in the Rain" and "I Concentrate on You" have the same four initial notes with the same time value. They are further identical in that both songs have a one-beat pickup note.

6. Even if their time values aren't, the first six notes are the same in "All of a Sudden My Heart Sings"; "Ghost of a Chance"; and "Surrey with the Fringe on Top."

The Copyright Office has other services available. If you have questions regarding songs, titles, or anything in this area, you may request research on that subject. Be specific regarding the data you desire. There is a moderate cost for this service ($10.00 per hour at the time of this writing).

This copyright information will give you brief practical knowledge. It is not by any means a legal opinion. Consult a copyright attorney who is an authority in this specialized legal field if you wish.

The best advice is: When in doubt, protect yourself and your song with a copyright.

CHAPTER TWENTY-NINE

SONGWRITERS' ORGANIZATIONS
or Don't Walk Alone

Performing rights societies are of inestimable economic importance to songwriters. The security they have brought us is the difference between living on easy street and the wrong side of the tracks. Talent, output, and fame notwithstanding, without the benefits we have gained through these protective agencies the majority of successful songwriters would not enjoy financial well-being as professional composers.

It wasn't always so. Before most of us inhabited this plane, these organizations did not exist. Songwriters lived on the sale of songs, haphazard (mostly hazard!) royalties from publishing companies, and had no protection. A song was considered to be in "open season." Bands could play it, orchestras could use it, and artists could perform it, all without any compensation to its creator.

On February 13, 1914, *The American Society of Composers, Authors and Publishers* (ASCAP) was founded. Victor Herbert was its prime mover. He recognized that the enjoyable products of composers and lyricists were used without fiscal reward to them. To correct this injustice, he gathered a group of songwriters in a call to arms against music users—theaters, cafés, dance halls, and wherever popular music was played. After a series of losing courtroom fights, the Supreme Court returned a verdict in favor of ASCAP. A musical composition was recognized as a property and its performance required payment.

A performing rights society is a licensing authority with a voluntary membership. It is a nonprofit association that authorizes music users to play the tunes—and pay for them—which are written by its members. It collects money from these users and distributes it to its members.

The requirements to join ASCAP are simple. A composer or

author (lyricist) must submit a copyrighted copy of his song which has been published commercially. A completed membership application form must be included with the music.

A composer or lyricist may become an associate member by submitting a copyrighted copy of his music or lyrics along with the application for membership. Publication is not necessary for associate membership. Annual dues are modest for either regular or associate membership.

Distribution is made to members based on these achievements and criteria: continuity, average performances, recognized works, current performances, and awards.

ASCAP conducts a continual survey of song performances on television, radio, and background-type music services. Payment is made quarterly to all members who have earned proceeds.

ASCAP has two separate categories of membership: (1) composers and authors (lyricists) and (2) publishers. Information stated here relates only to us as composers and authors, and not to the publisher category.

Additional information and an application for membership may be obtained by writing ASCAP at One Lincoln Plaza, New York, New York 10023.

Broadcast Music, Inc. (BMI), was founded in 1939 by a group of broadcasters. Soon composers and lyricists who felt the need for another licensing association to protect their musical property rights joined them. BMI is now a well-established major society, highly recognized in this country and in many parts of the world.

BMI essentially performs the same services as does ASCAP. It acquires rights from authors, composers, and publishers, then represents them as it grants licenses to perform its entire music collection to music users. Except for operating expenses, all proceeds are distributed to its voluntary membership.

Independent surveys are taken of music played in movies, radio, and television. In addition, symphony orchestra programs are studied to credit BMI composers for these performances.

BMI publishes a payment schedule of performing rights and royalties to each new member. Payment is made quarterly for U.S.

and Canadian performances, semiannually on foreign royalties, and annually on concert performances.

You are eligible to apply for membership if you have a musical composition which has been, or is likely to be, performed commercially.

Additional information and application blanks are available by writing BMI at 40 West 57th Street, New York, New York 10019.

There are a number of things which both of these performance rights societies do *not* do. They provide no legal advice, will not promote a member's music, will not assist in publication, nor find you a collaborator. Their sole purpose is to protect and distribute the performance income to which you and your song are entitled.

Another organization which has aided us is *The American Guild of Authors/Composers* (AGAC). Since 1931, it has been a watchdog for royalties due songwriters. In that year nearly a half-century ago, several "names" in our profession championed a cause for a standard and universal agreement with music publishers. Every contract then with a composer was a different sign-it-and-take-your-chances situation. This hit-and-miss document was "miss" more often than not for a songwriter. We, at that point in time, had little experience in either the legal or business end of music; there was scant background information for us to judge the fairness of any such legal agreement.

Billy Rose, Edgar Leslie, and George Meyer recognized our pending need for protection. Four attempts by them were fruitless. Another effort found fifty composers banding together to establish a basic composer/publisher contract.

The Songwriters' Protective Association was formed. Its name was changed to its current title in 1958, and over 1,400 publishers now recognize this organization, its members, and its standard contractual form.

AGAC proudly boasts of these services which it offers its members:

1. Provides the best writers' contract available.
2. Collects royalties.
3. Manages a copyright renewal service.

161

4. Issues a bulletin with essential songwriter information.
5. Administers writer-publisher catalogs.
6. Conducts "rap" sessions.
7. Provides a collaboration service.
8. Maintains a composers and lyricists educational foundation (CLEF).
9. Operates an estates administration service.
10. Has song or catalog financial evaluation.

There are over 3,000 members of AGAC. They include contributors to American music in every phase—pop, rock, folk, concert, country, jazz, theater, motion picture and television scores, and commercial jingles.

Two types of membership are available: (1) associate member (as yet unpublished) and (2) published composer. The former pays modest dues. The latter pays dues based on his or her royalty income.

AGAC has collected over $1,500,000 in royalties for songwriters that would otherwise have been lost. It has been of very real financial benefit to its many members through the years.

For additional information and a membership application, you may write AGAC at 40 West 57th Street, New York, New York 10019.

You should be familiar with one further organization: *The Confédération Internationale des Sociétes D'Auteurs et Compositeurs.* That grand French title is translated as *International Confederation of Societies of Authors and Composers* (CISAC).

This association has no individual members. It represents the various societies of authors and composers for protection within its international framework. That it does so is stated in its current brochure: "Through its 90 member Societies and Organizations spread over the five continents CISAC unites and represents more than 300,000 authors and composers belonging to 45 countries."

There is no requirement for a composer or lyricist to join any of these associations. If you are not writing music for financial gain, they will serve no purpose except the pride of belonging to such an organization and the remote-distance fellowship with other songwriters.

If your on-the-chart hits are not returning the income which you think they should, join the 19,000 composers and lyricists in ASCAP, the 30,000 BMI members, or some 3,000 songwriters in AGAC.

Don't walk alone.

I. CHEERS!

CHAPTER THIRTY

PREPARATION FOR PUBLICATION
or Have I Done *All* My Homework?

At last we come to that rewarding moment which every songwriter hopes for—publication. You are about to join the ranks of the talented tunesmiths who have enjoyed success from their creative abilities. You envision the fame and fortune awaiting just around the corner. You picture that gold record hanging on your wall, the people standing in line to buy your song, the interview in your newspaper which reads "Local Composer Makes Good with Good Music," and the president greeting you as you enter his bank. These are your exciting dreams which are about to become realities.

You are ready to be published. Are you sure?

Before your name might become a musical legend from coast to coast, let's make certain that it will. Are you *really* ready to go public? You will be more secure in our musical jungle if you have completed *all* your homework. Give yourself this examination as you mentally answer these questions:

1. You wrote your song. You rewrote it, then rewrote it again, making little improvements each time. You played it back on your tape recorder. In fact, you played back several versions of it.[1] You listened to it in both the cold

---

1. The best recorded help consists of making three or four cuts of the song back to back. This allows you to hear it without stopping to rewind the tape often.

Suppose you have two different versions of the song. Even if they are slight (a variance in the melody line of only several notes, or the choice between the words "sunset" or "sundown"), listen repeatedly to both of them. Either alternate these versions on tape, or make several takes of the first version followed by as many cuts of the second rendition.

Keep your lead sheet and lyrics handy. Study them as you listen, and make improvements.

Any time is a good time to give full attention to each dotted eighth note and lyrical comma. While shaving every morning for three weeks, I

light of day and the romance of shadowy twilight. You were brutally analytical, cutting and changing to improve your song.[2] The result: the best product of all possible versions, your smooth and all-but-published can't-miss song.[3]

2. You gave your song the "girl-friend test." Frankly, that isn't worth much. After all, she likes everything you write, especially if you wrote it for her. But she may offer suggestions, and she might like it just slightly less than your other songs you played for her.[4] If nothing else, her affirmation that you are a creative genius (you knew it, of course, but it is nice to hear again!) will give you more confidence in your song before the cold business world of musical publishers takes a hard, unbiased look at it.

3. Then you put it through the "neighborhood test." That examination may be no more conclusive, being kindly rather than critical. Your neighbors have a prejudice: they like you, they want to like your song. An additional bias is that you are probably the only composer within miles, and they point with local pride to you.

---

listened to the several versions of each song in my score for Peter Ustinov's magnificent play, *Romanoff and Juliet.* If my lead sheet was water-spotted and my chin occasionally nicked, each hearing proved to be a valuable session.

2. I wrote the script and score of a musical comedy with a San Francisco setting entitled *What's a Few Years?* After giving it every test for several months, I scrapped the entire score of nineteen tunes and made it into a straight play. Why? Instead of adding to the play for the enjoyment of the audience, the music seemed to slow the action and pace of the show.

While this is vastly different from cutting a word or a note in a song, it is a lesson to be learned: I have never missed anything I cut from a play when it got into production. As creators, we tend to regard our every pencil mark as irreplaceable. Such is not the case. Be honest with yourself; delete what isn't vital, change what you can improve. The results will merit this action.

3. I spent an entire month on a single song. It had thirty-four different versions! While many of these were slight, they evolved into six distinct melodies. Much time was required in refining it, and it proved to be well worth the effort.

4. Read Meredith Willson's book, *Eggs I Have Laid.* An episode regarding the playing of a new song for his wife, her comments, his rewriting, and her help with less-than-enthusiastic early approval are both a lesson and humorous reading.

If, however, they are candid, you may get a fair opinion. Since they are the butcher, the baker, and the candlestick maker, they are also the man on the street—listeners, appreciators, and buyers of popular music. Those are the people your song must please for its commercial success.[5]

4. Next, you gave it the "bounce it test." You "bounced it" off anybody else you could think of, particularly knowledgeable authorities. If they don't fully qualify for that title, they are at least learned people who understand the creative art form.

To this forum you want to listen v-e-r-y closely. What did the bandleader say? How did the disc jockey react? And your friend, who is a real pop music fan? The music store owner's opinion? And the record collector? You considered their advice, and either took it or didn't. But you searched them out to listen, heard their ideas patiently

---

5. Remember the adage: Songwriters don't bleed. If you ask for a frank opinion, be ready to accept honest criticism. When a new play has satisfied the tests prescribed here, I invite my actor friends to read parts and make comments. We critique after every scene. On one such occasion, I was told: "If I were in your audience, I'd go out for a smoke right now because I am bored." He went on to explain why. Analyzing his advice later, I found that he was correct. I deleted the unimportant opening to *Give 'Em Hell, Harry!*, and started the play two scenes later.

Such critiques may include these remarks: "The pace seems too slow, the plot doesn't move forward, the dialogue doesn't fit a character's personality, the scene just doesn't track." Every suggestion must be considered. If several people make different comments regarding the same scene, perhaps none of them are right—but something is drastically wrong. That scene deserves real study to correct it. The same is true of your song.

Even if suggestions are no more specific than "I get a general feeling," that is worth your reappraisal. It may be the same "feeling" that the public will have. Comments are based on what people hear, not what you intended but apparently didn't get across. Use these well-meant recommendations to your best advantage.

and without argument, and then made up your mind regarding their suggestions.[6]

5. And finally you gave it the "best test": Is this the *very best* I can do? Is my song now in optimum form? Does it say what I want it to say? Does it sing what I want to sing? Does it meet every category on my work sheet?

Your answer must be a resounding *yes*. If it isn't, you are wasting your time. Don't spend the money and effort to try to get it published. Don't jeopardize your credibility with publishers on a less-than-perfect song. (Remember, you will be contacting those same producers again with future songs.) You must go back and prove your song affirmatively against every criterion in these tests.

And so your answer must be—and finally is—*Yes!*

Now you prepare a very smooth lead sheet, type highly legible lyrics, get up a good demo, copyright your song (if you feel it is necessary), and send it to publishers and record companies. You do so with full confidence, knowing that your song is as perfect as you can possibly make it. Then you can forward it with this:

"Here is my song. It surely has every chance of being a hit, because I have done *all* my homework!"

---

6. On my thirty-days-in-April/thirty-four version song, several of those versions were sent to a disc jockey, a poet, and a local author. They all are creators or authorities. Their opinions were especially valuable.

7. If you don't recall that helpful item, refer to chapter 2: "Tools."

CHAPTER THIRTY-ONE

PUBLICATION
or Welcome to the Winner's Circle!

Your song has mastered each test and received "bravo!" responses from every listener. Now to get it published. The question is...how? Fortunately, that riddle has a lot of answers.

There are a number of different ways in which songwriters have succeeded in finding an enthusiastic publisher. Most of the time, none of them achieve results. Sometimes some of them work. Now and then, they all do.

We have discussed the odds of the songwriting game. The chances of making a return on our investment of creative time and talent are worse than the odds-against-us gambling casinos or the race track. But we wouldn't be songwriters if we were easily discouraged. We don't want to hear about the ninety-nine out of a hundred songs which don't get published. We have faith that ours is that special song which will find success. So let's get back to the question: How do we get our song published? Here are several avenues:

1. **If you know a well-known group's manager, you are in rare good luck. Send him your demo, lead sheet, and typed lyrics, then sit back and relax; your friendship will practically assure you that your song will be heard by this stellar group. (Who you know can move mountains—and help make hits—in the music business, too!)**

2. Send your song to disc jockeys. They listen to demos, depending on how much time is available to them.[1] If

---

1. One disc jockey—a friend—listened to a new demo of mine after first finding it in the *eleven* demos he received that same day! Guess how many he heard? Guess what he did with the others?

you have a personal acquaintance at a radio station, chances are you will get a hearing. If you are a well-known writer with past success, that will surely give you a leg up. If you have a friend who is a friend of the deejay, ask him for an introductory phone call. Without such an inside track, just mail it. . . and hope.

3. Invite a local musical group to perform it. If they like your material, they can help provide a following for it. They can develop more interest from a local audience for a song by a local tunesmith rather than that of a songwriter miles away.

   Should they establish public acceptance for your tune, you have a definite advantage when offering it to a major recording company. You can relate your local success story and the acclaim which your song has received. Most music producers try area markets before they make the much larger investment required to go "national" with it. You have already proved an acceptance in one market, and its positive result is important.

4. Send it to big-name stars or their agents. Unless you have a personal contact, your chances of being heard are niller than nil. Star names, addresses, and agents are printed from time to time in show-biz periodicals.

5. Make personal calls on publishers. The major ones are located in Nashville, New York, Los Angeles, and Chicago. Your experience with them will run the entire gamut:

   a. An A&R (Artist and Repertory) man will listen to your song with you and comment on it. (Don't expect a yes-or-no answer; he must present it to a committee for approval. At least he may give you his opinion at that time.)

   b. You will be dismissed with the remark that an executive will hear it soon and report to you within a few weeks.

   c. You will be told that this firm is concentrating on Latin or soul or country (too often the "sound" your song isn't), but thanks anyway.

   d. This publisher is overloaded with new material for the next six months, and there is no point in leaving your song, but good luck.

More often than not, you will receive a reply from them. While it is not a for-sure, the presumption is that the publisher listened to it. He needs a continual stream of new material and must consider songs presented to him. In virtually every case, you will find a courteous welcome. And that, in itself, is encouraging.

6. Publish your own material. You can establish your own recording firm (a relatively simple matter). Consult an attorney so that you don't encroach on another firm's name, then obtain musical performers and make a good recording. Be prepared for some expense. Unless you have a sharing agreement with musicians, this can cost you a minimum of several hundred dollars.

   Now you are ready for the market. Send or take your record (and it must be a highly professional product) to record stores, radio stations, and publishers. Maybe you can make some money in your local stores. Of course, your real goal is publication with a major company. Advise those publishers that your song, the master of your record, and perhaps the contract of your recording group are available to them. If your song, marketable record, and performers are quality, this method can save a publisher much expense.

7. Write and compose a theatrical musical. It requires you to become a playwright, or find a playwright who is interested in collaborating with you on such a venture.[2]

This unique event is interesting. About 1960, an enterprising songwriter rented billboard space in New York. On it was a copy—ten feet tall—of his lead sheet. Above it, he addressed a message to Perry Como (or was it Dean Martin?). It read to the effect that "my song is right for you, here it is, please consider

---

2. This idea motivated me to write and compose my first musical comedy. Rejections from publishers were rampant on my demos. Hoping to find a solution to the no-thank-you-but-good-luck experience, I wrote book, score, and lyrics for *Double Double*. If it did not make stage history, at least it was the only original play produced by Kansas City's Circle Theatre.

it, and contact me." The trade magazines carried stories about this innovative effort, and interviewed Como/Martin (?), who said he would get in touch with this inventive chap. What happened? No information is available in spite of my efforts to find out for you.

Try these approaches to market your to-be-a-hit song. All of them do work at some time on some songs, which is how our fellow composers get published and find success. There is no ironclad formula, no surefire solution for publication. We ask only an opportunity, and these are the many routes for it.

Once more we offer this advice: Don't be discouraged by a courteous rejection. There remain other publishers to be heard from. Even if the last one declines, that is no reason to pawn your guitar, burn your piano in the fireplace, vow that you will never send out another song, or put a pox on the business end of the music business.[3]

Keep your song. Be patient. Write another tune, and another. Give them your same effort toward publication. Music tastes change. So do personnel in publishing firms. In two years—or three, or five—send that first song back to those same publishers. The verdict then could very well be successfully different for you.

Many standards have survived an earlier rocky road. "Stardust" is an example. Meredith Wilson's musical comedy, *The Music Man*, was finally at the right place at the right time to make it legendary musical theater; that triumph came after many rejections starting twenty years earlier.

If you have talent, perseverance, and the character to stand ninety-nine rejects, you have every qualification deserving that one loud happy *Yes!* Isn't it worth trying—and trying again—and waiting for?

Then we can congratulate you with our enthusiastic "welcome to the winner's circle!"

---

3. My Conservatory student was ready to do all of the above. I suggested the try-it-one-more-time approach. He did, and Ken Russell's "All Because of You" was released by Liberty Recording in 1977. Incidentally, the title was given to all students as a writing assignment. Ken's splendid song got him a recording contract out of his homework.

CHAPTER THIRTY-TWO

WHY SONGS DON'T GET PUBLISHED
or Better Luck Next Time

We have all been disappointed to receive a polite form rejection slip from a publisher. And we were totally astonished. How could they make such a mistake? "I'll show those birds when my song is a hit!", was our reaction. Do so. We're for you!

Now let's take a look at why our material was turned down. It could be any of the following:

1. Poor demo recording.
   a. The accompanying musical background is too loud.
   b. The melody line of the song isn't clear.
   c. The chart is too fancy and over-arranged.
   d. It is unprofessional—scratchy, out of balance, and difficult to hear.
2. Inferior lead sheet.
   a. It is illegible and hard to read.
   b. It doesn't parallel the demo recording.
   c. It lacks chord symbols and/or typed lyrics under the melody.
   d. It is musically incorrect.
3. Tune.
   a. It is unimaginative, unoriginal, uninteresting, and plain "vanilla."
   b. It is far out, too unconventional.
   c. It isn't pretty.
4. Lyrics.
   a. It either tells a poor story, or tells a good story poorly.
   b. Its rhyming is forced, dull, and unappealing.
   c. The song topic is overworked, routine, or commonplace.
   d. The words are not catchy, without thrill or excitement.
   e. Coherence/plotting is lacking.

5. Title.
   a. It is uninspired.
   b. It has too many words.
   c. It is not repeated often enough to be retained.
6. Form.
   a. It is not AABA, ABAC, or ABAB.
   b. It is AABA, ABAC, or ABAB, but not correctly so.
   c. It is an unusual form (ABCD, or other), but not a good enough song to overcome the difficulty of using this uncommon pattern.
   d. Its "B"/bridge doesn't release a listener from its "A" phrases.
   e. Its overall structure is inferior and unappealing.
7. Miscellaneous.
   a. Typed lyrics were not included with the demo and lead sheet for the publisher to follow as he heard the music.
   b. Song was not copyrighted, and a publisher would not risk a nuisance lawsuit.
   c. You didn't provide a return address by which the publisher could contact you.
   d. All items (demo, lead sheet, typed lyrics) were unprofessional in both appearance and sound.
8. Rules compliance.
   a. You failed to conform to the specifics of hits we have stated.
9. Other.
   a. You sent it to too few publishers.
   b. You wrote a great song, but had it at the wrong place at the wrong time.

Many of us have been "guilty" of that last condition. Don't use it as an excuse. If your song is truly great, then it and you should persevere. A year or so from now you should try again. Hopefully you will be at the right place at the right time with the right material. We will sing your song—and your praise!

Meanwhile, follow these suggestions. Show those publishers. We don't want to wait to hear your song. You won't need better luck next time.

CHAPTER THIRTY-THREE

THE SONGWRITER'S STYLE
or Broaden Your "Musical Signature"

Stop reading, close the book, get a pencil and paper. Sign your name ten times. Now look at it. Every signature is almost identical.

Most songwriters have a "musical signature." Our songs may tend to have a similarity about them. The explanation is simple: We "hear" songs better in one key than in others, one form comes more naturally to write in, one chord progression tends to fall into place, and one rhyme scheme is easier for us.

We may even have several different "signatures"—one for AABA, another for ABAC, and a third for ABAB. That is progress, but still not what you want. Perhaps we have a "signature" in rhyming, in the bridge, in tags, or with certain lyric words. In each of those several content areas, we have a tendency toward alikeness.

Don't worry: those symptoms are occupational. We all have them. Fortunately we can do something about it.

Some songwriters' musical mannerisms are easier to spot than others. Authorities can recognize songs by certain composers and lyricists because of these natural habits. It is not that their songs all sound alike; they definitely don't. But their composing tendencies are identifiable.

In my opinion, Frank Loesser and Cole Porter varied their musical "signatures" more than any other songwriters. The teams of Kander and Ebb, and Newley and Bricusse have unrestrictive styles.

The collaborative combination of Martin and Blane also has that rare ability of making every song sound unique, distinctive, and dissimilar. Perhaps one of the reasons is that both write lyrics and music.

To illustrate the broad "signature" by which this songwriting team is blessed, we analyzed five of their outstanding songs in the various categories, contents, and areas. Note each heading and the dissimilarities found in these songs.

Title	Key[1]	Form	Tempo	Time	Bars[2]	Chords[3]	Words	Title Words	Title Location	Title Stated	Verse/Bars	Tag	Rhyme Words By Phrase
"Ev'ry Time"	F	ABAC	slowly	4/4	32	19	100[4]	2	up front	6	yes/22	No	A: toes/nose B: tree/sea A: shock/knock C: mark/dark
"Buckle Down, Winsocki"	F	ABABCAB	march	6/8	56	10	116	3	up front	1 "buckle down" 5 "Winsocki" 5 "down" 4 (1 + + + + + + + + + + + +)	yes/34	No	A: down/down B: wrecks/necks/hex A: yell/hell B: in/win/chin C: defeat/retreat A: down/down B: down/town/crown
"You Are for Loving"	F	ABACt	slowly	4/4	38	28	60	4	in bars 25 and 26	1 "and loving" 2 (1 + +)	yes/16	6 bars	A: ringing/bringing/clinging B: spinning/winning A: humming/strumming/coming C: you (none) t: do (none)
"Have Yourself a Merry Little Christmas"	C	AABAt	slowly	4/4	38	22	92	6	up front and go out	3	yes/8	4 bars	A: light/sight A: gay/away B: yore/more A: allow/bough t: now/(none)
"The Boy Next Door" [5]	Bb[6]	ABAC	moderate	3/4	32	27	57[4]	4	go out	3	yes/36	No	A: ignore/door (say) B: please me/tease me/sees me (way) A: heart-sore/door (display) C: adore/ignore/door

---

1. Stated on sheet music.
2. Not including verse but including tag.
3. Chorus only.

4. There is entire optional repeat of chorus with new words.
5. Second stanza is for a boy singer and reads "the girl next door."
6. Verse is in F, chorus transposed into B flat.

We see that not all five songs differ in every category every time. We do, however, find these many variables: three keys, two forms, three tempos, three rhythms, three song lengths, different chord totals (10, 19, 22, 27, 28), varying word quantities (57, 60, 92, 100, 116), title words (2, 3, 4, 4, 6), changing title locations (three are "up front," one is both first and last, one is "go out," and only one appears in the middle of the song), varying title repeats, different verse lengths (8, 16, 22, 34, 36 bars), two tags, and no rhyme words appear twice except for rhyming the A and B phrases of "The Boy Next Door" ("say") with the second "A" in "Have Yourself a Merry Little Christmas" ("gay").

And there you have, music lovers and songwriters, real variety by a great songwriting team.

How can you broaden your music-writing techniques? The work sheet in chapter 3 will help. Even if you aren't writing a musical score, the chart listed in chapter 27 will be of further assistance.

Stop reading, close the book, get a pencil and a new sheet of paper. Write your name ten times, forcibly creating each different from the others, and yet all must be legible for anyone to recognize what you wrote. Make the letters taller or smaller, plain or fancier, wide or narrow, bold or shy, straight or slanted, and otherwise and other ways. Now look at your page. Every writing is no longer a signature, and nothing is identical . . . except that you wrote them.

That's what you want in your music—your inventiveness, your broad approach, your ability to create in every musical color of the rainbow—and it still has *you* in it.

Difficult? Not really, but it takes some concentrated work. You can do it with your music and lyrics. Of course: you just did it with your name.

Make a determined effort with every song. Do something different: Change key, form, be "wordier" or less so, put the title in an unusual place for you. We all have a natural style in everything we do. Depart from it. Develop a new "signature"—or many. Stretch your ability and vary the sound of your songs. Broaden your "musical signature."

CHAPTER THIRTY-FOUR

POTPOURRI
or That's French for "Odd-Lot Advice"

We have been together now from "welcome" through "congratulations," studying and enjoying our exciting creative field. In thirty-three chapters we have attempted to cover all musical and lyrical areas, and to share practical information. If you have learned, we have succeeded.

Now let's review, summarize, emphasize once more, and look again to provide you with every suggestion and idea. We don't want to leave any musical note "undotted" or a single lyrical "t" uncrossed to help you along the road to successful songwriting.

♪ The making of a demo needs thorough planning. Be certain that it has a quality sound. Before you spend time and money, here are several important points for you to consider:

1. Most publishers like reel-to-reel demos, preferably cut at 7.5 ips (inches per second). Wax demos are acceptable; the speed of 45 rpm (revolutions per minute) is best. Cassettes are less popular.

2. Your recording must be clear and audible. It need not be cut in a recording studio with super equipment and electronic tricks in ultra-fidelity. However, a listener must be able to hear your lyrics and follow your melody line.

3. A demo may consist solely of a good vocal rendition and basic (piano/guitar/organ) accompaniment. It doesn't have to be fancy or fully orchestrated. If you wish, include additional voices and instruments for a more sophisticated sound. The important thing is a clear understanding of your words and music.

4. The demo label should include your song title, name, address, and phone number. List its playing time in minutes

and seconds. State copyright information if it has been either applied for or received.

5. Make three cuts of the song if there is time and space. They may not be heard. At least there is the opportunity to hear it twice again. If your song plays immediately before the listener reaches for the "off" button, he might hear it one more time. Repetition in hearing your song is important to retention, just as it is in the title and other parts of your tune.

6. When mailing your demo, include a lead sheet and typed lyrics. The listener hears your song from the demo while seeing it in print for additional clarity and understanding.

7. Include postage if you wish the addressee to return your demo to you.

8. A brief letter explaining the mood, tempo, form, why your song is "right" for a specific publisher (based on his current releases and performers), and your thanks for his consideration. This letter should be an original rather than a duplicated copy.

Employing these suggestions can make your song stand out among many other demos, and not just waste a publisher's time.

♪ If you run out of gas, so to speak, in composing, get a fresh start. Write in a new key. That approach is of further value when the key is a more difficult one for you. Explain it we cannot with any logic, but we "hear" different harmony/melody/chords/ideas in different keys.

You also might change moods, forms, tempos, rhyme schemes, and rhythms. They can rescue you from a sameness if you are becoming a little stale in the key of F with all upbeat numbers and a 1, 1, 2, 2 rhyme pattern in the AABA form. Refer to the work sheet in chapter 27 ("Writing a Musical Stage Score") for a review of this subject.

♪ Never *sell* a song. Allow, by written contractual agreement, its rights, use, and performances. Under every circumstance, keep title and ownership of it. There are too many instances where a composer sold a song, only to have it become a hit, then be revised years later with a big popular demand again. That songwriter may have received a decent price originally, but its new owner is en route to the bank!

♪ We don't—fortunately—hear much about them anymore. A generation ago, "song sharks" preyed on the novice composer. They promised fame, fortune, and a rags-to-riches overnight success to anyone knowing middle C from Y flat who could rhyme "moon" and "June." These con-game promoters ran ads in many publications, assuring instant triumphs. *The Reader's Digest*, and others, exposed them. Still they remained relentless on an innocent public that had lofty ambition, too often scant talent, and a lot of hope.

My "shark" experience is singular and brief. A fly-by-night producer recorded my songs on a single 45 rpm. He secured some radio time and got us a following. Inviting me to his office, he suggested that I advance $300 so that we "could hit the European market while making the charts here." My answer was fair, firm, and friendly: No thanks! Regrettably, he conned the young vocalist of those sides into agreement. He has not been heard from since.

When reputable publishers feel that they have a potential hit, they finance and promote it. If they ask you, the songwriter, for front money, they are neither legitimate nor do they care if they have a hit. The only "hit" they have in mind is you!

Your contribution toward a successful song is your creative talent in the song itself. Don't—repeat *don't*—contribute your bank account as well.

♪ That denizen is not to be confused with legitimate musical services. Many firms offer demos, arrangements, collaborators, and lead sheet publication. For a stated fee, they provide what they promise.

How do you tell the difference? At the outset, be sure that what you will get is what you pay for. If you doubt the publisher, ask for references from him, write the Better Business Bureau where he is located, and require a signed contract before sending money.

♪ This may help in the mechanics of your composing. On my first rough draft of a song, I color-code for additional clarification: lyrics are typed, the melody is scored in a soft (No. 2) lead pencil, chords are in red, accidentals/incidentals/instructions and copyright data are in blue, lyrics are in green or brown or purple. A handful of colored pencils is worth having.

♪ The argument is ever old and never-ending: Are words or music the most important ingredient in a song? Either can be and has been. We know of countless examples where superb lyrics made a routine melody into a hit, or a magical tune which overcame a very average jumble of words. I have read opinions by musicologists that "Londonderry Air (Oh, Danny Boy)" is probably the most attractive melody ever written, and that "They'll Never Believe Me" is the ultimate blending of words and music.

♪ Stay consistent in your song form. The audience anticipates with pleasure a duplication of the melodic line and rhyme pattern of your opening "A" phrase in the following "A's". Don't disappoint your listener or he will disappoint you—by losing interest in your song.

♪ A new songwriter must be better than the established song-writers. His material has to outshine (outsing?) that which is currently heard by his well-recognized and now-applauded peers.

This is the same competition faced in the sports world, for instance. A rookie tries to make the team. To do so, he must excel over an established player, the guy who was good enough to be in the lineup last year. Every season we find players who are. So it is in the music game. That "rookie" who makes the starting musical lineup could well be you.

♪ Lyrics are copyrightable only under the category of "book" or "periodical." Unless you have several lyrics to compile under such a heading, the single lyric must be part of a song to enjoy the security of a copyright.

♪ Copyrights are transferable. They may be assigned to another person or firm by a simple agreement of both parties.

♪ You can surely add songs under every category we have studied here. Space was our only limiting factor. The tunes we analyzed provided the best examples of those areas.

♪ What is the best songwriting motivation? That's easy: fall in love. I wrote Jane twenty-two songs in the first fifty-eight days I knew her. That shows what an inspiration falling in love can be! Look at the wide-open horizon you have under that happy condition, and these self-explanatory titles:

"You Came Along"
"When I Met You"
"Lonely Was I"
"You Changed My Life"
"Don't Ever Go Away"
"Now That We Are Together"
"We Could Be a Habit"
"Forever with You"
"Don't Ever Leave Me"
"I'm Lonely Without You"

These possible titles are a plot in themselves: meet, greet, like, love, and perhaps lonely, if it doesn't work out. P.S.: With Jane, it happily did!

♪ If you can write a song, you can also write commercial jingles. This area has proved financially rewarding to many top composers. Explore this possibility with advertising executives in your area. Whether they pay a one-time fee for complete use of your tune or residuals with royalties each time it is used by the broadcasting media (markets differ from city to city), this field can be beneficial to you.

♪ A famous inventor offered the secret for his success. It was amazingly simple:
1. Determine a need for what has yet to be invented,
2. Invent it,
3. Be patient for public acceptance of your invention.

How like inventing is songwriting!

♪ We have seen examples where music was written prior to the lyrics, and where words came before they were set to music. Here is a unique approach: Cole Porter often wrote the beginning and ending of his songs, then completed the middle portion—working his way from both the top and bottom.

Only once did I divorce myself from starting at the top. I had an idea for the last lyric line: "When I fall in love again, once again I'll fall in love with you." Then I built the song backward, leading up to this clincher. Unusual, yes; but it might work for you, too. Any approach is a good approach as long as it achieves results.

♪ Probably the sole composer of a college song to continue his collegiate success was Cole Porter. While many others tried to duplicate the campus fame their fight songs achieved for them, the indefatigable and ever-ingenious Porter found it. "Bull Dog . . . Eli Yale" was the first of his many great hits.

♪ Are you lost for a melody to fit those lyrics running through your mind? Try this: Play the C chord on the piano with your left hand, then hunt and fiddle around with your right hand through a series of notes—any notes. As the musicians say, you are just "jamming" in the key of C. If you find the beginning of a melody, then play the F chord, and more at-random notes. If that works, repeat the process with the G chord. Note that you stayed with "family" chords. Now you are beginning a successful search for a melody, "prospecting" in music for something that fits. And, of course, retain your efforts on a tape recorder.

♪ The old adage that "your first inspiration is the best inspiration" is right more often than not. It may need to be refined. It may even take off on a different direction as you work to improve it. But it was the beginning germ from which you can polish. This fact also makes a case for not losing it; you have it on tape, don't you?

♪ Playwrights say that they must write to a definitely structured outline. If they don't, a character can "run away with the play," changing its course of action in a manner and direction that the author hadn't considered.

When I first heard this, I regarded—and disregarded!—it as folklore and romantic folly. When it happened to me, I found that it is true.

Sometimes it can be advantageous, offering a new plot direction not previously considered.

Did your song arrive at the conclusion you planned for it? If not, was it a better ending than you had originally intended?

Songs can change direction too, both for better and for worse. It rarely happens because there is not the almost-human element of a play's character to "take charge" of a song.

This is not to suggest that every song needs to be scenarized in the sense that a play is. But it is a good idea to have a general outline of your song's plot in your mind.

♪ Wake up and jot it down—now! Make the effort, take the time, do it! I have done so, and woke up the next day happy that I did. Too many times I didn't, thinking that I would write it in the morning. My promise was honest enough, but my muse had taken a vacation; there wasn't any inspiration there to write. Don't be comfortable, sleepy, and lazy. Squint into the bright light, find your pencil and paper, turn on your tape recorder, and compose. You'll like tomorrow better because of your discipline and the rewarding beginning of your new song.

♪ From our informal dictionary, we should understand two words:

1. *publication.* This, for us songwriters, is not just printed words and music on white paper. Its legal definition is the distribution and/or exhibition of a song in any form: records, transcripts, tapes, radio and TV presentations, performances. If you give a lead-sheet copy of your song to your neighbor, it has, in technical terms, been "published."

2. *standard.* Music grammarians like to debate this term. It has always meant those songs which are formal and near-classical, such as "Trees," "Stout-Hearted Men," "The Road to Mandalay."

For our purposes, a standard is a popular song which is a perennial, always in demand, ever blooming, continually heard, and a permanent part of America's music. "Night and Day"; "The Trolley Song"; "Embraceable You"; "Blue Skies"; "Tea for Two"; and "All the Things You Are" are standards by our definition here.

♪ "Will my song be a hit?" With hope in our voice, we always ask ourselves—and anyone else who will offer an opinion. (My answer to myself is "certainly!", and I'm inspired to write another "hit." At least they are all potential hits to me!)

A songwriting friend once told me that he could always tell which new song would gain such status. Of course he can't! If he could, he would be too busy writing his own hits to do anything else. And if he could pick winners for publishers, think of the expense they would save. He could have made a million dollars, or is it a million dollars a day? His crystal ball isn't that good; nobody's is.

You answer that question. Your tune is great, your lyrics plot, you followed all the rules, and your song is appealing. We hope that you are at the right place at the right time, and the public replies with a resounding *Yes!*

♪ The grammatical purists would fault us lyricists. How many songs have the phrase "you and me" when "you and I" is correct? That would get us a zero in our next English class, but it may be just the right line in a song.

We even, on occasion, use awkward sentence structure. For example, "Forever is not long enough, my love for you to tell." It says, "Forever is not long enough to tell you of my love." The lyricist used it for rhyming purposes. Because it is a great song which we applaud, we forgive him—and enjoy—his misplaced verb.

Poetic license is a privilege of the lyricist. Use it infrequently, carefully, and skillfully—and know what you are doing when you break a basic grammatical rule.

♪ Of many sophisticated lyricists, probably the kings of the turn-of-phrase were Cole Porter and Lorenz Hart. The latter wrote "I'd go to hell for ya, or Philadelphia." His "Manhattan" is equally clever.

♪ Censors, critics, and public sensitivity have dictated to us tunesmiths what we can—or mostly, cannot—say in our lyrics. Shakespeare wrote in bawdy times for the public mood. Since then, the pendulum has swung toward purity. Look at what this century has done in a let's-clean-up-our-songs discipline:

In 1910, "Every Little Movement" was thought to be highly suggestive. Originally banned, it achieved popularity a generation later.

"Let's Put Out the Lights," in 1932, had its next lyric line changed from "and go to bed" to "and go to sleep" because of the obvious connotation.

"Rum and Coca-Cola" was a big hit in 1944. However,

a disc jockey had to announce it over the air as "Rum and Soft Drink." To sing "Coca-Cola" in the song was apparently fair; to state "Coca-Cola" was some sort of taboo.

Where are we now in song "sanitization"? Back to the very frank end of the pendulum's arc. Subjects today include dope, illegitimacy, unmarried cohabitation, divorce, prison, booze. Except for some four-letter words, virtually anything else is permitted.

♪ Song length? We discussed it, and it is worth another look. Not including verses, but including tags, here is a review:

"Happy Birthday"	8 bars
"My Ideal"	16 bars
"Once in Love with Amy"	20 bars
"Moonlight in Vermont"	26 bars
most popular songs	32 bars
"My Funny Valentine"	36 bars
"Chattanooga Choo-Choo"	40 bars
"Moonlight Serenade"	44 bars
"Cabaret"	56 bars
"Love for Sale"	64 bars
"Soliloquy"; "The Trolley Song"	many bars

♪ This topic is debatable. Most creators find it is easier to write music to words than put lyrics to already-composed music. If you disagree, we will agree with you. Whatever works for you is the best practice.

♪ A former shipmate claims credit for this approach. An outstanding Navy leader, Captain Bob Beskind has a brief self-imposed priority. He calls it "The KISS Rule," or "Keep It Simple, Stupid!" We can profit from his advice. Let's borrow that "KISS" for another suggestion: Keep It Singable, Songwriters!"

♪ We have briefly mentioned "musicians' songs." What are they, and why?

186

Musicians' songs invariably have an uncommon sound, both in melody and harmony. They often change key.[1] They allow for improvisations, making them fun to play.[2]

Lyrics do not make, nor hinder, a musicians' song. The message is not important; the melody and the chord structure are.

Nearly all of them fall into the "standards" category because of their public popularity. Many—most?—are financial successes. It is well worth your while to study these songs and discover why they rank among the favorites of professionals who play them.

This list is by no means complete: "Once in a While"[1]; "Body and Soul"[1]; "April in Paris"; "Night and Day"[1, 2]; "Spring Can Really Hang You Up the Most"; "Gone with the Wind"[1]; "Tea for Two"[1]; "How High the Moon"[1]; "Stella by Starlight"; "All the Things You Are"[1]; "Pennies from Heaven"; "September in the Rain"; "Ja-Da"; "C Jam Blues"; "I Only Have Eyes for You"; "Moonlight in Vermont"[1]; "When Sunny Gets Blue"; "A Portrait of Jenny"; "I Got Rhythm."[1]

In the mechanics of writing lead sheets, you may wonder when the stem of a note goes up (♩) or down (♩). At B above middle C the note stem can go either way. Obviously, every note below it "stems" up; the notes above B "stem" down.

I write all treble-clef (which is the clef for all popular music) note stems up on lead sheets, regardless of range. This technicality—up or down—isn't important, as long as the song is legible.

---

1. These songs have key changes.

2. During the summer of 1947, I played piano with a trio at the Last Chance Saloon (no kidding). It was in Kansas City, right next to the state line, and was the last chance to get a drink before going into then-dry Kansas. The place was a neighborhood bar without frills; its constituents were a meat-and-potatoes assemblage with draw-beer and fundamental music tastes.

One night there were few dancers and no requests. We could play what we wished, as long as it wasn't too far out. We did: solo followed improvising solo in real playing enjoyment of "Night and Day" for forty-five minutes.

♪ Do you "cheat" yourself when composing? Many songwriters do, including the man here. Because we have a keen sense of chord structure and harmony, we can make anything from the cheer of a baseball crowd to the noise of a train wreck sound pretty.

For that reason, we should be careful not to cheat. We should write the melody line only, then put in our chords. If one-note-at-a-time sounds good to us, we know that this fundamental melody is correct before adding to its appeal with handsome-sounding chord harmony.

♪ We purposely stayed away from this topic when we discussed "Chord Formation" in chapter 20. Now that you understand all about chords, let's look at "chord voicing." Essentially it means the predominate sound that comes out of a chord.

For example, when we strike a C major seventh chord, we get its true sound if it is voiced:

But if we invert those same notes to this order it becomes "cloudy" and not at all the clearly-voiced sound we intended.

In a major chord or "triad," meaning three notes, we can use those notes in three different positions/orders.

Here is the C major chord: This is called the "root position." The notes of the chord as they naturally occur in the scale—C, E, G.

This is the "first inversion" of that chord. The same notes now have new positions. The first note (C) becomes the top note, and the middle note (the third of the scale/chord E) is on the bottom. The harmony doesn't change, but its "voicing" does with a stronger sound of C at the top.

Here is the "second inversion": Its changed position of the same notes provides another variance from what we saw—and heard—in the root position and first inversion.

A chord is a chord. But to "voice" it with these available "inversions" will provide a little different sound to improve the harmony of your songs.

♪ The number of songs in a musical play and their reprises have a fairly wide range. (See chapter 27, "Writing a Musical Stage Score.") The plays chosen for this survey were twenty playbills and programs picked at random from my private collection. They are:

Play	Number of Songs	Reprises
Good News	18	2
A Little Night Music	17	0
The Magic Show	12	0
Pippin	15	0
Over Here	15	1
Irene	14	1
1776	12	1
The Merry Widow	16	1
By the Beautiful Sea	18	3
The Pajama Game	18	4
The King and I	15	2
Wish You Were Here	20	2
Paint Your Wagon	22	2
Can-Can	20	1
Plain and Fancy	17	0
Annie Get Your Gun	17	0
Kismet	15	2
Peter Pan	18	2
South Pacific	16	0
Damn Yankees	14	1

The average number of songs in these plays is over sixteen, with reprises at one plus. Seventeen songs and two reprises seem to be a good guideline for our musical theatre efforts.

♪ You observed in the song "Pretty You" in chapter 3 that

189

chord symbols are written for each *new* chord. If the C chord, for instance, prevails through two consecutive bars, it is written only over the first bar. There is no need to write "C" over the second measure; a performer knows that a chord applies until changed.

In chapter 21 ("Chord Progression"), we didn't follow that rule only for the sake of full illustration. Your lead sheet doesn't need such "clarity." Write the chord symbol only when a new chord is necessary.

♪ Chapter 11 ("Lyric Word Quantity") urged lyric brevity. We do so again, with this to-the-point limerick:

> There was a young songwriter, Jos.,
> Who said, "I cut lots, maybe mos'.
> There's much I don't need
> And that's why I succeed;
> My songs aren't so wordy, verbose."

♪ We see an occasional song with its title followed by parenthetical words. Cole Porter did so with his ingenious "Let's Do It (Let's Fall in Love)." Is it a three-word title, or seven? Does Jerome Kern's "Long Ago (and Far Away)" have two or five words in its title?

I have never heard this issue debated, probably because there are few academicians to discuss it, and it is not a do-or-die matter. But our Conservatory class did, long and hard. The general (but not unanimous) opinion is that only the "unparenthesized" words make up the title.

Why was the subtitle/additional phrase necessary? Students wanted to know. Did the composer feel that the title was incomplete without it? Was clarity needed? Did a publisher, perhaps, suggest it?

I can't answer for others, but my own experience may be informative. The first line of my song is "This is the last time I'll ever fall in love." That ten-word phrase is much too long, even if it is what the song is all about. "This is the last time" was the obvious up-front title. But "the last time" for what? The equally important point was "I'll ever fall in love." That phrase *had* to be included.

What did I finally do? I titled it "This Is the Last Time (I'll Ever Fall in Love)," and I consider it a five-word title.

I felt that it needed the subtitle explanatory phrase.

The parenthetical subtitle—if that is what it is, and that is as good a definition here as any—is a legitimate convention. Use it, as others have, if it will benefit your song.

♪ This won't help you write your next hit, yet it is a salute worth sharing. My neighbor paused his lawn-mowing to wipe his brow and visit over the back fence some years ago. A fan of both popular music and the Boston Red Sox, he made this pronouncement: "There are three great Americans— Ted Williams, Cole Porter, and Ella Fitzgerald." That two of them have been major contributors to our field is high tribute.

♪ We have discussed melodic contrast, motion, and direction. The song, "Lover," is one of the best examples. This 1933 Rodgers and Hart hit had a popular reincarnation for a new generation of fans in the 1940s by the swinging Gene Krupa Band.

In its "A" phrases, it employs chromatic motion, and descends in its melodic line. The "B" ascends, providing an interesting and contrasting bridge in this AABA song.

♪ Did you ever write a song, only to be befuddled, and have to ask yourself: "What the heck key am I in?" Two clues will tell you:
1. your last chord, and
2. your final note.

If you are writing in the key of C, C major (or perhaps C6) will be your final chord. And, not counting fancy arrangements or voicing, the last note in your melody will be the tonic/C.

♪ What you write and compose is what we hear. In helpfully analyzing a song in our Conservatory class, the message of a songwriter wasn't clear to the other students. The young composer explained that "the point I made was. . .". But he didn't make that point.

There isn't time for an explanation. Write what you mean, make certain that it is right, and mean what you want us to sing.

♪ Has it all been done? Not by a wonderful chance it hasn't!

191

Look at what has been accomplished in a generation: Put a television set in your living room, gave your kitchen a dish-washer and a freezer, air-conditioned your house, let you ride a power lawn mower, permanently pressed your clothes in your own dryer, gave your car a telephone and a CB radio, and added two more United States. After making new discoveries and advancements in every known field, we even put a man on that moon you write songs about!

Not by a long shot it hasn't been done. Nor has it all been sung. Nobody has written your next new and different song. Nobody will till you do it. So do it!

Where do you go from here? What is your next step to improve that rare gift of talent with which you are so fortunately blessed? We offer these suggestions:

1. Study further. Read every available treatise on songwriting.
2. Perform your songs and get reactions. Determine why they are liked by your audience, or discover what caused just a polite reply.
3. Read the show-biz journals. See what is making musical news.
4. Listen to the radio to hear what the public currently appreciates.
5. Watch the charts. Find out which songs have a following and analyze them.
6. Critique your own songs for lyric and musical merit. If they don't live up to your expectations, consider collaboration with a fellow creator which might be mutually helpful to you both.
7. Get more knowledge. Take piano or guitar lessons or a course in harmony.
8. Write another song and another and another. Begetting begets begetting. The more you write, the more ideas come to you, and the better your writing becomes.

Have we said it all? I hope so.

We have addressed every category of our unique and exciting field. We have offered rules, statistics, hints, ideas, and examples of songs which made our peers successful. We have added our personal experience. We have quoted from the greats and the quotables. And we have attempted to make your songwriting hobby or career all that you want it to be.

Our single premise was stated many pages ago—to make better songwriters of you who have that magnificent gift of creation.

A professor kept a highly talented student after class. I overheard him say to this promising standout: "Your construction form isn't the best, and your mechanics need work. We can improve them, and you can learn. But you have imaginative ideas with a fresh creative spark. That is what pays off."

We hope that you also have that same spark.

And so we close with our "tag": Good wishes to you for fun and success. May you achieve your goal in our exciting world of words and music.